Afghan children's drawings (pages 1–11)

FAZAL SHEIKH

THE "VICTOR WEEPS"

AFGHANISTAN

Scalo Zurich – Berlin – New York

AFGHANISTAN is a country inhabited by numerous peoples of diverse regional, cultural, linguistic and religious affiliations. According to the last census made in 1979 the population was 13 million, 40 % of which are estimated to be Pashtun, 22 % Tajiks, 15 % Hazaras, and 5 % Uzbeks. Some three-fourths of the population are Sunnite Muslims and about one-fourth are Shi'ite Muslims.

The Pashtun mainly inhabit the southern and eastern parts of the country. Pashtun means Pashto-speaking, the Persian designation "Afghan" being applied chiefly to the western tribes, while "Pathan", the Indianized form of the native name, is used for the eastern ones. Therefore, the Pashtun bore the exclusive name of Afghan before that name came to denote any native of the present area of Afghanistan.

The Tajiks, about 3.5 million, live predominantly in the north-east and in the west around Herat. Their language is Dari, a Persian dialect spoken by about half of the Afghan population. About 1.5 Million Shi'ite Hazaras of Mongolian ancestry inhabit the central mountains of the Hindu Kush. In the plains of northern Afghanistan Sunnite Uzbeks are the largest population group.

Situated at the intersection of three geographically and culturally distinct worlds — India with its monsoons, Central Asia with its steppes, and the Iranian plateau — Afghanistan has seen a succession of invaders and colonizers. It was conquered by Alexander the Great, after his death it came under Seleucid and Indian control and was then subject to Hindu influence. In about 870 Islam became firmly established. The Mongols under Genghis Khan invaded the country in 1219, and after their empire fell apart, Afghanistan lay partly within the Mughal empire of India and the Safavid empire of Persia.

The different peoples and ethnic groups enjoyed a semi-independent status until the end of the 19th century. Even though Nadir Shah and his successor Ahmed Shah Durrani consolidated Pasthun rule over Afghanistan and united it in 1747 as one country — for the first time under its name Afghanistan — it took more than a century to accomplish central rule in the reign of Abdul Rahman (1880–1901).

In the 19th century Afghanistan was plunged into strife and tribal feuds and became a buffer state between Czarist Russia and British India. In three Anglo-Afghan wars (1839–42, 1878–80, 1919) Afghanistan lost territories in the north and west but secured its independence. The Pashtun heartland, however, was divided in 1893, half of it forms the North West Frontier Province (NWFP) in present-day Pakistan.

From the 1920's onward Afghan rulers began reforms — including constitutional and administrative changes, allowing women not to wear the veil and the establishment of coeducational schools — provoking the opposition of the conservative religious and tribal leaders. In 1953 traditional leaders supported Mohammad Daud Khan in becoming prime minister — the same Daud who seized power again in a coup against king Nadir Shah in 1973.

As prime minister and later as chairman of the newly established Republic of Afghanistan, Daud took a stronger line on Pashtunistan, forcing the idea of independence of the Pashtun tribes in the NWFP. The relationship with Pakistan and the United States deteriorated. Although Afghanistan refused to take sides in the Cold War, Daud turned to the Soviet Union for economic and military assistance.

However, in the late 1970's he tried to move Afghanistan away from its dependence on Russian aid. But Soviet influence over the social, political and military elite of Kabul had become paramount. The two communist parties reunited in opposition to Daud and seized control of the government in 1978.

Their Marxist reform programs sparked major rebellions and, finally, the jihad of the Mujahedin. Soviet troops invaded Afghanistan in December 1979 to prevent their Afghan allies from being overthrown. Ten years later the Soviet Union withdrew its 100,000 troops and the last communist government of Mohammed Najibullah was brought down by the Mujahedin in 1992. A provisional Islamic republic was established.

The Mujahedin militias are composed of different ethnic groups and get financial and strategic aid from regional and international powers competing for influence in Central Asia: For many years Pakistan — together with the USA and Saudi Arabia — supported the Pashtun militia of Gulbuddin Hekmatyar to promote a new relationship to the Pasthun people. Iran continues to align itself with the Shi'ite Hazaras and the Persian-speaking Tajiks under their Commander Ahmed Shah Massoud, and the Uzbek General Abdul Rashid Dostum fosters the contact to the country's northern neighbor Uzbekistan and his old ally Russia.

Ethnic and personal rivalries between the victors of 1992 caused new and prolonged combat. Most of Kabul, including the old city and the central bazaar, has been reduced to rubble by factional fighting.

In 1994 the Taliban emerged. In their majority they are Pashtun students from schools set up among Afghan refugees in Pakistan during the years following the Soviet invasion. By September 1998 they had conquered 95 % of Afghanistan.

In 1990 the refugee movements came to a peak: almost half of the Afghan population — 6.2 million — had fled the country. By 1997, 2.7 million Afghans were still living in exile, about 1.4 million in Iran and 1.2 million in Pakistan. In the 20 years since the Russian invasion circa two million Afghans have been killed.

Text provided by the publisher

KYRGYSZTAN

UZBEKISTAN

TURKMENISTAN

DUSHANBE

TAJIKISTAN

CHINA

Mashhad

Mazar-e Sharif

Baghlan

IRAN

Herat

Bamian

Chitral

Laghman Konar

②①

KABUL

AFGHANISTAN

Jalalabad Timergara

Lowgar

③

⑧ Peshawar

⑥

Ghazni

Paktia

ISLAMABAD

Khost

④

⑤

⑦ Miram Shah

Kandahar

Paktika

North West
Frontier Province
(NWFP)

Lahore

INDIA

Quetta

Refugee villages:

Urghuch ...1

Khairabad ...2

Ghazi ...3

Bizen Khel ...4

Ghandi Khan Khail ...5

Akhora Khattak ...6

Miram Shah ...7

Badabare
and Nasir Bagh ...8
(in the surrounding of Peshawar)

PAKISTAN

15

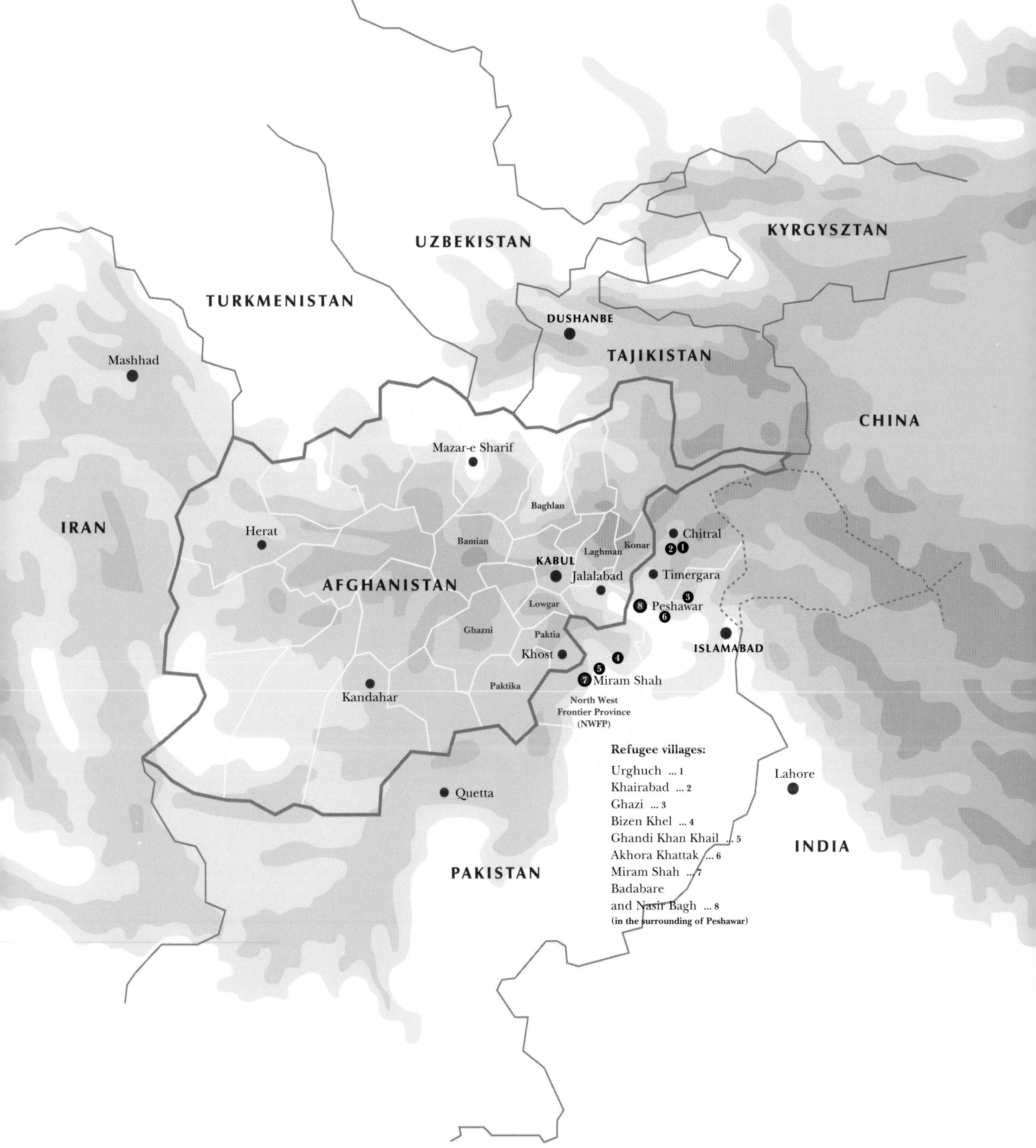

The peoples became part of the faith,
but were erased.
So if the victor is weeping,
O people of the world,
only look at these cities,
that have turned to desolation.

Mirza Asadullah Khan, Afghan poet

Kabul cityscapes, August 1996, one month before the Taliban conquest of the city (pages 16–33)

غازی محمد عثان خان

بنیاد فرهنگ

Seekers of fame more base than able
have lent this world the face of hell.
A hundred times blood wets the earth
as some son of a nobody grows famous.

Rahman Baba, Afghan poet (1907–1987)

United Nations High Commissioner for Refugees (UNHCR) camp for "internally displaced persons", Jalalabad (pages 34–35)

TO SHEIKH FAZAL ILAHI, the grandfather I never met
but for whom I am named. Although you died in 1955,
I have witnessed the greatness of your legacy in the gentle and
kind demeanor of your son, my father, Abdul Majied Sheikh.

Haji Nadir

THE LAND OF AFGHANS

In the ochre evening light, the muezzin leaves his home and makes his way through narrow passageways toward the mosque. Children playing in the alleys greet him along his route. For a moment he stands, surveying the empty courtyard, before climbing the worn rungs of the ladder to the roof. There, hands cupped beside his face, he intones the 'azan, the call to prayer. The thread of his singular voice, frayed by decades of these evenings, flows across the courtyards and down the gullies to the farthest recesses of the village, entering the houses and stirring the people within.

This was our first night in the Afghan refugee village of Bizen Khel in northern Pakistan. Our host, Mohammed Omar, the headmaster of the school, sat cross-legged on the ground before us, a pot of green tea at his side. Next to me was Abdul Sattar, my friend and interpreter, who would travel with me across Pakistan and Afghanistan, and through whose generous spirit I would come to know the Afghan communities. In a corner of the room, Mohammed Omar's youngest son, only slightly bigger than the pitcher of water he carried, silently placed his burden beside the door before vanishing into the private recesses of the house and his mother's waiting arms. As the sound of the 'azan wound through the open window above our heads, we had lapsed into silence, and as the call came to a close, Abdul Sattar and Mohammed Omar began their ritual cleansing in preparation for the evening prayer.

Minutes later we strolled together down the pathways towards the mosque. In the distance, the courtyard was now full of life as men moved through the archway exchanging greetings. Old men, steeped in centuries of Afghan history, huddled together in conversation, propping themselves against the outer walls. From time to time members of the group would rise, gathering their robes about them, and vanish through the darkened entrance. When we neared the mosque, I split off from my companions and stood watching at a distance as Abdul Sattar approached the villagers. They smiled approvingly, greeting a fellow Muslim with hospitality, ushering him into the security and camaraderie of their brotherhood. I watched until they had closed around the new visitor and disappeared into the mosque, then continued down the path, glancing through a side window at the worshippers within. Treading cautiously, I followed the path down a steep gully which opened on to the banks of a stream where children were playing a round of cricket. I sat beside the stream, staring into the waters rushing at my feet, taking a few moments of quiet contemplation of my own, and wondered if there was any similarity between my calm meditation and the solace these men received from prayer.

When I came back up the path, Muslims were flooding the courtyard, slipping into their shoes and readjusting their leggings. Seeing me they crowded around, greeting me with both arms extended in the most gracious and genuine of all Afghan greetings — a sign of welcome and equality, an embrace reserved for close relations. They studied me carefully and asked my name. As I recited Fazal Ilahi Sheikh, "Grace of Allah", a murmur spread through the crowd. My grandfather's name, now my own, one so foreign and strange in the United States where I was born, provided an immediate entree into this community. The men whispered to one another and nodded in recognition and acknowledgment: "musilman," a Muslim.

One of the elders — who I later discovered was Mohammed Omar's father — silenced the rest as he reached out to touch my cheek. He told me that he knew I was a Muslim because he could see a spirituality in my eyes most non-Muslims lack. He grasped my hand and, drawing me with him, led the elders away from the mosque back down the path to his son's house and the gathering of the *shura*, the council of elders.

The elders of Bizen Khel are ex-Mujahedin, freedom fighters who fought in the jihad — the holy war — against the Soviets, and who have lived in exile, just across the border from their own country for nearly twenty years. In the past, these men had responsibility for acting as judges in Afghan society, their decisions were binding and final. Now, in these refugee villages, they keep the spirit, traditions and hierarchies of Afghanistan alive, coming together each evening to discuss the events of the day.

In the warm cocoon of the room, illuminated by a gaslamp, their wizened faces flushed with color as they told stories from their Afghan villages. They talked

Shahzada

of the bombings, the Soviet occupation and the *shahid* — the martyrs killed by infidels in the holy war. The bodies of these martyrs, buried beneath the earth they once tilled, are like sentinels in the minds of their countrymen, leading them along the route which will one day draw them home.

The jihad against the Soviets has been over for almost a decade. But what should have been a victory quickly spiraled into civil war as rival factions of their own Mujahedin began a power struggle which has destroyed the capital city of Kabul. In the latest round of fighting the majority of the country was captured by the Taliban — literally "religious students" — who imposed their own interpretations of Sheria, the body of Islamic law. The movement which claimed to bring security and a just Islamic state has become increasingly repressive and divisive. Women have been forced to leave their jobs and schools, and brutal beatings are imposed on civilians for minor infractions. There is neither a consistent policy to govern the country, nor economic means by which to alleviate the desperate conditions, and as the residents of Kabul grow increasingly alienated by the regime, there is a growing feeling that they will return their support to the Mujahedin and their bid to regain power. But when these villagers talked of their homeland, they still expressed a remarkable degree of hope. Though their optimism seems largely unwarranted, their spirit still persists.

On the periphery of the room, a young man of nineteen, who had only recently gained entry to the *shura,* sat listening, enraptured by the stories. After the elders have returned to their families, it was his duty to prepare the room for sleeping. He introduced himself as Masafer, which means "traveler", and told me something of his life. He was born in 1979, only days after his parents fled their homeland to Pakistan, and had spent his whole life in exile. Afghanistan — "the land of Afghans" — is a place he visits only in his imagination. As he spoke about his country I recognized the cadence of longing in his voice, not for politics or society but for something more intimate and less grand. It was a child's need for the touch and sensation of an animated history, the desire to inhabit a place that only exists in stories brought to him in the flickering evening light.

As we lay down to sleep in the cool air, the spirits of these stories kept vigil over us. In their dreams, Masafer and the other Afghan refugees would be lured from their beds, beyond the walls of their homes, up into remote mountains that divide reality and memory, home and exile.

Gholam Nabi

Abdul Mohammed

Sheikh Fazal Ilahi (ca. 1953)

MY GRANDFATHER

Several years ago, during a stay with my family in Kenya, my father gave me a photograph of my grandfather, Sheikh Fazal Ilahi. It is the only picture I have ever seen of the man who died ten years before I was born. He sits before the photographer gazing into the camera, and so, to me. All the stories that I have heard about him, as well as those from my own imagination, have become part of the way I view this portrait. In his costume — turban, pressed suit and tie — Islam meets the modern world. But it is his expression that reveals his character, his lifelong idealism and religious devotion.

Sheikh Fazal Ilahi was born at the turn of the century in what was then northern India: partitioned in 1947, the region where he grew up is now Pakistan. Like many others of his generation he emigrated to colonial Kenya in 1912 and worked as a merchant in the small town of Nairobi. While he and his fourteen-year-old bride carved out a life for their growing family, the town blossomed into the thriving capital of Kenya. Although he had never received a formal education, my grandfather became a successful entrepreneur and bought large tracts of land in Nairobi. The proceeds of this endeavor provided for the family and enriched the community, satisfying Islam's requirement that each individual contribute a portion of his earnings to the welfare of society. He established philanthropic trusts for the poor, for education, and for charity, and thus nurtured respect for the Sheikh family name within the Muslim community and throughout Nairobi.

In keeping with his faith, Sheikh Fazal Ilahi performed the *hajj*, the pilgrimage to Mecca, traveling overland through the tribal areas and desert of northern Africa and on to Saudi Arabia. It was an arduous journey requiring negotiations with tribal leaders for safe passage. He bought a house in Medina to be closer to the holy city of Mecca and the birthplace of the Prophet Muhammad. Although I have never been to Saudi Arabia, I have seen pictures taken by my father of his own pilgrimages. One of these photographs, taken from the upper tier of the Prophet's shrine, looks out across the mass of Muslims encircling the

Ka'aba. I imagine my grandfather flowing among the worshippers in continuation of a movement begun fourteen hundred years before, the devotees treading a path to eternity.

In 1955, during a trip to his third wife's family in Syria, Sheikh Fazal Ilahi died of a heart attack. It was his wish to be buried in Medina, where the family of the Prophet Muhammad was buried. Muslims believe that when the Prophet rises from his crypt, so too shall those buried in Medina. With the intervention of the Saudi Prince Faisal, permission was granted for my grandfather's body to be flown from Syria to its final resting place.

Eight years later, my father traveled from his university in the United States to visit his father's grave for the first time. He had not been to Medina since he was a small child. On his arrival, a neighbor led him through the streets of the city into the cemetery. Although headstones are forbidden by law, the neighbor had marked the grave at the time of Sheikh Fazal Ilahi's burial by driving a stick into the ground, and so my father stood beside his father's remains among the unmarked graves of Muslims in a land he did not know.

During my childhood in New York City, part of each year was spent away from home visiting the family in Kenya. There were sprawling compounds of uncles and aunts and a wide-reaching family network. To my child's eyes this place, both far away and completely home, was full of raw beauty and boundless freedom. At night, my father enthralled me with stories of his childhood and the Sheikh family glory in the city and surrounding countryside. When his reflections turned to memories of his father, his voice grew respectful and distant. Since my grandfather's death, the resources of the philanthropic trusts he created have been depleted, the houses have fallen into disrepair and the reputation of a once-respected family is in decline. Now when I return to Kenya, it is difficult to find connections to the grand history I learned of as a child.

I am my grandfather's namesake and though I can never know him, I continue to search for part of him to call my own. He is in the Pakistani folk songs my stepmother sings, and in her father's Urdu poems, set to music, from which her hypnotic voice draws out the latent emotion. Finally in 1996, in the desire to know him better, I followed him back to Pakistan. By visiting the land of my fathers, moving through the space linking the present to the past, I hoped to gain insight into who they were and by extension who I am. In Pakistan I discovered that the

Asudullah

land had been settled by hundreds of thousands of Afghan refugees, who had lived in exile during two decades of war in their homeland across the border. They welcomed me into their midst, and for two years I returned to the refugee villages to share their stories of loss and endurance. In allowing me to record them and photograph them, they relived their memories of their homeland, and voiced their hopes that they would one day be able to return.

One morning, in an Afghan village north of Timergara in Pakistan, our host's son brought us a radio to hear the news. As he sat proudly holding the radio on his lap, the neutral tones of the announcer brought the world's events into our room. One story reported the discovery of a mass grave near the northern Afghan city of Mazar-e Sharif in which more than two thousand corpses of Taliban fighters had been found. The following story reported the Taliban government's denial of aid to provinces around Bamiyan, where famine threatened thousands of civilians, because the Taliban believed the convoys of relief supplies might fall into the hands of opposition groups. Later, as I walked through the exiled community, I read the emotional reality of the news on the faces around me.

Turning away from the streets, I followed a path that led to the archway of a mosque. I removed my shoes and stepped inside. The prayer-ground was encircled by carved wood columns which vaulted up to a stone roof to join sections from an earlier Buddhist era, the two religions melding into one. For a moment, all talk of religion, violence and society vanished. I moved to a corner of the courtyard where I sat while Muslims came and went. From this vantage point I could see the devotees padding across the carpet of pine needles in bare feet; I could feel the sensation of the needles on the soft base of my foot. The worshippers proceeded to the cleansing pool where they poured cool water over arms and feet, cupping their hands to raise an arc of water to the face and ears before it trickled back to its source.

All around, Muslims prostrated themselves. One man stood and performed the *nemaz*, the offering of prayer, passing his hands to either side of his head, encircling his ears, while his neighbor bent toward the earth. As though the offering was being passed, one man finished his *nemaz* as another began. The people before me appeared invisibly joined, with only the sound of the water and the rustle of clothes to break the silence.

In a corner of the mosque where tombs from the last century nestled beneath carved beams, a young boy sat with a Koran propped between his knees and an old man sat at his side. As the boy's hand, dwarfed by the enormous book, followed the verses he recited them aloud, and from time to time the old man leaned over to instruct him. I studied the old man's face. In it I saw something of my grandfather. Sheikh Fazal Ilahi was sitting across from me, and the boy by his side, earnestly struggling with the words, was my father. If I could have asked them about their lives, what would they have told me?

While I sat in the grotto the sun began to set. The old man gently removed the book from the young hands and rested it upon his lap where he wrapped it in cloth. I rose from my spot and moved over the needles to the door, the noise of the pool guiding me through the darkened passageway. When I reached the entrance I slipped on my shoes and stepped back into the anonymous streets.

Gholam Sadiq

Dad Mohammed

Nasruddin

LETTER FROM THE ELDERS AND COMMANDERS OF
THE AGRA DISTRICT IN LOGAR PROVINCE

In 1979 the Soviets and their communist minions attacked our country of Afghanistan,
our village and its people who love Islam beyond anything. We had our own religion and
culture and we rose up in unison against the communist regime. We started a jihad with
our traditional weapons and the mullahs and the *shura* gave us direction. In the months
that followed, the Soviet troops terrorised our people and many of our mullahs and leaders
were killed. There were frequent bombardments and massacres. Often, it was the sound
of the dogs barking that gave us some warning. The usual method of attack was for the
helicopters to begin the operation while the tanks and land troops followed. We knew that
helicopters arriving was a sign of more to come and we would flee our villages and take
refuge in the caves in the mountains. Hundreds of innocent civilians were murdered and
many more injured. Even today our villages and our crops remain in a state of destruction.

They thought that they could silence us, take away our heart. But they misjudged
us. The people of my nation are unique in our hospitality, bravery, dedication and
willingness to sacrifice. These attacks only strengthened our resolve and the jihad spread
throughout the country. Afghans can only agree with a Muslim state. Our ultimate goal
was to expel the Soviet infidels and establish an Islamic government with Sheria law.
The same holds true today. In the following decade of Soviet occupation, thousands of
our people were murdered. Our religious leaders, scholars and philosophers were beaten
and abducted. Some of our national leaders were imprisoned while others were killed.
Many simply disappeared and were never heard from again. But we did not surrender.

We knew our families must be taken to safety until peace had returned to our land.
Our tribe, which is known as Ahmed Zai, decided to migrate through the White Mountains
to Pakistan. We left all our belongings behind and began the long journey through the
desert and mountains. We traveled at night to evade the soldiers, but they could detect
our movements. They knew the routes we were using and many of our people were lost
during bombing raids at night.

After settling our families in Pakistan, we men returned to fight against the Soviets
on a tribal basis. Ours was the third district to be liberated from communist rule. Several
of us were commanders of the Mujahedin forces in our area. We gave up our homes, our
belongings and our lives because we believed in the jihad. No one instructed us to fight.
It was our duty as good Muslims. If it were not for our religion, we would not have had to
flee from our land. I know that none of us can forget even a single stone of our villages, but
our dreams are stronger for a country under true Islamic rule than they are for the loss of
our homes. If I am willing to sacrifice my life and the lives of those in my community for
this ideal, the loss of our homes is of little significance.

As a result of all of our fighting, the communists were defeated. The Soviet Union was broken and their troops ousted. Our people were saved from the harm of communism. Then Mujahedin groups took possession of Kabul. During this period, our hearts were nearly exploding with happiness. We began to make preparations to return to our village. But we did not see any happiness. Fighting between the different Mujahedin factions followed and we became disheartened. We learned that the commanders were not waging a true jihad to establish an Islamic state. Greed and the desire for personal power is not consistent with the aims of the jihad. We lost hope in the future of the Mujahedin movement. We withdrew our support and returned to our families in Pakistan. We no longer wanted to return to our country.

When we reflect on the years of war, we know that we followed the true message of the religion. Even if we were required to do the same things a hundred times, we must faithfully engage in the jihad. We were not the ones with power to make the ultimate decisions. It is the Mujahedin leaders who did not carry out their duty. When we begin to fight one another, we lose sight of the true meaning of the jihad. Perhaps power has forced those commanders away from their religion. Although we are saddened by the outcome, it is beyond our control.

Countless people in our country have been killed, but most of the countries of the world were deaf and blind to our plight. If there is a car or a train accident in another country it will be announced around the world and other countries will know about it. But about the victims from our country who were killed fighting to save the world from communism there is not a word. Why has our community been forgotten by the United States and the United Nations? Even today some countries are interfering in our internal affairs but the rest of the world remains silent. We are depressed and upset. We ask that the surrounding Islamic countries and the United Nations not interfere in Afghanistan's affairs with their own aims at heart but that they bring all the Muslim people to a peace table so that Afghans may live in their own country.

We have our own national, Islamic and tribal traditions with which to solve our internal problems. These kinds of decisions are not popular in the other countries of the world. The problem now is that the Taliban are not willing to share power with those who can help them sustain and broaden their government. The Taliban represent the final hope of the people. If those that we have put our trust in as mullahs are unable to bring peace and security to our land, then the future remains bleak. The window of hope is beginning to close. But we believe in Allah's mercy and that there will be a day when we can return to our village. With stability, we will happily return. I look forward to that day, for many of our children and young adults have never seen the land which their forefathers gave their lives to liberate.

Haji Hasan, Haji Durani, Fateh Khan, Haji Guger, Haji Amrose, Aftar Mohammed,
Saleh Mohammed, Qaher Khan, Haji Bualijan, Wajan Khan, Surgul —1996

Gul Mohammed

Rohullah

ROHULLAH

In 1981 my cousin, Qari Monir, which in our language means "one who knows the Koran by heart", was taken along with thirteen other elders and mullahs by communist troops into the desert. For six months the villagers did not know what happened to them. Then one day a shepherd minding his animals in the desert area surrounding the village saw a piece of white cloth under the earth. He pulled at it and finally he realized that it was a long scarf. As he continued to dig he saw that there was a man buried there. He ran to the village to tell the people of his news. The villagers returned to the spot and began to dig. Eventually, the fourteen bodies of our leaders were recovered. Their hands and feet had been tied and they had been buried alive.

Even though it had been six months since their deaths, their bodies had been perfectly preserved — the mullah even had on the glasses he was wearing the day he was taken from his home. These were spiritual people and they were awaiting a proper and respectful burial. It was this incident which convinced us that the communists were willing to kill us all, not just those who were fighters. And so we decided to leave the village and take our families to the safety of Pakistan. In the months that followed, the men returned to Afghanistan to free our country from the invaders.

ABDUL RAHMAN

I watched from the top of the mountain as the communists destroyed my home. I said aloud, "Alhamdu li'llah! — Praise be to Allah! — They cannot break our spirit."

Abdul Rahman

Samar Gul

When I was young, I wrote poetry about love,
beauty and peace in Afghanistan.
Unfortunately, at this age, I write about the tears,
the blood and the cries of the Afghan people.

Ustad Khalillulah Khalili, Afghan historian
(b 1905)

MOHAMMED OMAR

When I was a child at school in Afghanistan, there was a large yard. Hundreds of us would gather there after school to play and talk with one another. When my schooling ended I was hired as sub-director in the district administrator's office. From there I became deputy mayor of the province. Soon the communists came to power and I was forced to leave my country. Now I am the headmaster of the refugee school here in Pakistan. Sometimes, when the students have gone home and I return to work, I sit in my office and look out across the playground. In those moments I remember my early days in Afghanistan and what I had to look forward to in the future. The war has changed many things.

Haji Nadir

NASRUDDIN

I am from the Konar province of Afghanistan, but I have lived here in Pakistan
at the Ghazi refugee village for the past eighteen years. In 1979, during the reign of
Babrak Karmal in Afghanistan, some of the Mujahedin started the revolt against the
communists. Our village of Kerala was on the route for these fighters as they made
their way from Pakistan into Afghanistan, where they would continue the jihad.
One day a commander by the name of Gulrang came to our village. He had been
sent to ask us to take up arms against the Mujahedin to stop them from using the
area as a thoroughfare. He summoned nearly eight hundred of the villagers to the
riverbank beside a bridge near Chaghasray where he was to address them. As is
our Afghan tradition, the women and children were left at home.

When he arrived, instead of speaking to the villagers, Commander Gulrang
had the communists surround the group. The villagers were first gassed, then
the order was given for the soldiers to fire upon the crowd. A boy who had been
standing on the bridge overlooking the riverbank watched as his father was
murdered. He ran home to tell his mother who had only recently given birth to
a new baby boy. When she heard the news of the massacre she lost her mind.
She remains crazy even to this day.

When the other women of the village heard of the massacre, nearly thirty
of them ran to the river and threw themselves into the water. They preferred to
be swept away by the current and to join their husbands rather than to be taken
by the communist troops. Most of the people of the village were killed on that day
but it is difficult to have an accurate tally of how many. The widows of Kerala who
escaped fled to Pakistan where they live together in a refugee village.

Commander Gulrang lives, even as I tell you this story, in Tirali village in
the Afridi tribal area. He lives even today.

Gholam Sahi

Abdullah

Gul Mohammed

Last night blossoming boughs were laughing,
swaying a lone iris and jasmine and laughing.
In the distance, I saw the lucky morning star.
At its own luck, and my life, it was laughing.

Rahman Baba, Afghan poet (1907–1987)

Sayed Ahmad

MAULADID SAID MOHAMMED

In 1981, during the Soviet-backed government of Babrak Karmal, my brother traveled from Peshawar to his home village of Bamakhil in Afghanistan. Many of his relatives and the elders of his area had gathered together for his wedding ceremony. Then, on the very night that he brought his bride to their home, a group of Mujahedin arrived in the village. They were on their way from Pakistan to another village further north.

My brother, along with other villagers, had to guard these men to ensure that they would not put the village at risk. So without having time to visit his wife, Abdul Mohammed took a rocket launcher on his shoulder and sat in a bunker all night long. In the morning he heard shooting. Afraid the communist troops were advancing, he left his bunker and ran to find out where the firing was coming from. He soon realized communist forces had surrounded the village, and there was no opportunity for him to return to his position. Then they began to fire upon him from a bunker. To save himself, he fired a rocket back and when the communists began to flee Abdul Mohammed pursued them. But as he passed the bunker two men raised themselves and began firing. They had been lying in wait. My brother was killed on the spot.

Abdul Mohammed never had time to see his wife, never had time to be with her. She had been selected for him by the families as he was living in Pakistan. As is our Afghan tradition, the husband first sees the bride on their wedding night. My brother never saw his wife's face. Later she was married to my younger brother, Abdul Rahman, and they now live in Ghazi refugee village in the North West Frontier Province of Pakistan. They have three children named Balqisa, Lalzamina and Hedayadullah.

My brother Abdul Mohammed was dearly loved by his people.

Mauladid Said Mohammed

I throw aside the rose with thorns.
Enough, I say, of the wine that stupefies.
Weary of a hundred years of this life
followed by a moment of silent shame.

Rahman Baba, Afghan poet (1907–1987)

Abdul Basir

Shabaz Khan (ca. 1978)

MAZARAK

Do not forget Shabaz Khan and the story of our home. We are from the Torakhail tribe which originates in the Paktia province of southern Afghanistan. Our village of Rajikhail was a peaceful community of religious Muslims who grew up farming the land. Then in late 1979 the Soviets began to take action against the Mujahedin in the south. They entered our villages and murdered our women and children, destroyed our farmlands and animals and left us without shelter from the desert.

Eventually we made the decision to leave Rajikhail at any cost. As we in the *shura* prepared the village for the migration, Shabaz Khan came before us pleading that he and his family could not leave their home. He had been born on this land and had spent his entire life in the village. He said what became of him and his family would be the will of Allah. With great sadness, we respected his wishes. Leaving our houses full of our possessions we made our way along the path that would lead us out of Afghanistan. As we pressed higher into the mountains, some of our villagers spotted Russian planes headed towards Rajikhail. We watched as the communists bombed our village and farmlands. When the planes moved on, we knew we had to return to see what had happened to Shabaz Khan and his family.

As we approached the village we could see our homes had been destroyed. In the rubble we found the bodies of Shabaz Khan, his wife, and their six children. It was a great risk to be in the village so we moved to a safe area until nightfall when we could bury the dead. There was only enough time to dig one grave for the whole family, and then we gathered over the bodies and prayed. We left before dawn and resumed our journey through the mountains to a new life in northern Pakistan. We have not returned since that day. I know that there are many of these kinds of incidents in Afghanistan, but we saw this with our own eyes and buried this family with our own hands. They were our neighbors.

ABDUL MANAM

We started our jihad in 1980 with traditional weapons. As we captured small posts from the communists, we began to use the Kalashnikov. One night in 1981, the year of my twenty-first birthday, our band of Mujahedin attacked the communist post at our village of Pharash Ghani. Nearly one hundred and twenty of us laid siege to the fort and more than fifty of our Mujahedin were killed. By morning we had taken the fort and captured forty communists including their famous Commander Gholam. As was our tradition, we brought the prisoners back to our base to decide their fate. We asked the other Mujahedin to speak out if any of the prisoners had been responsible for the deaths of our people. The soldiers told us that they had been forcibly conscripted by the communists. Since no one testified against them, we agreed to set them free with the promise they would not return to fight for the communists.

When it came to Commander Gholam, we found he was directly responsible for the deaths of sixteen of our people. The brother of one of the men he had killed was given a rifle and Gholam was executed with one shot to the head. By morning, word of the night's events had reached the village at Saripul. By early afternoon three men, Abdul Ghafur, Laj Mir and Shad Mohammed, sent messages that Gholam had been responsible for deaths in their families and thanked us for bringing him to justice. But an informer must have sent a message to the Soviets because that afternoon they came to Saripul and took those three old men from their homes. They tied them by the legs and fastened the ropes to the back of a tank, then drove the tank through the main city of Kishem district as an example for the people. When their relatives went to the base to collect the bodies for burial, only the legs remained.

Abdul Manam, 1981

Abdul Manam

Shamsuddin

SHAMSUDDIN

We had heard of attacks in other villages but we thought only Mujahedin strongholds were being targeted. Then one morning in 1985 our village of Donighori was surrounded by communist troops. They threw a grenade into our neighbor Mohammed Akbar's house and he, his wife and four children were killed instantly. We fled to the mountains. Twelve of our people including a two-year-old girl were hiding in one cave. The Russians found them and they were all murdered except the little girl who was bayoneted and left for dead. We found her in the cave when we began to retrieve the bodies of our martyrs. She was taken to the hospital and eventually recovered. Today she lives in our refugee village in Pakistan.

After this we traveled for twelve nights until we reached Pakistan. At that time there was no refugee camp near Miram Shah and we had to spread out along the border. Soon after our arrival, the communists made a bombing run and one hundred and fifty people were killed. After this we were given refugee status and our families settled in the new camp at Miram Shah. Then we were free to return to Afghanistan and join the jihad.

We were fighting near the front in Baghlan province when eight Soviet jets began bombing our forces. I was manning the anti-aircraft gun. I could see the bombs as they dropped from the planes killing many of our fighters, yet I felt no fear, only anger. A long time before, I had decided to dedicate myself to the cause of Allah. I knew if I was killed I would become a *shahid* and bring great reward on myself and my family in heaven. In the middle of the battle a shell landed beside my machine gun and blew me from my post. When I regained consciousness in the hospital, my right arm had been removed and I had a deep wound in my right thigh. Weeks later I was brought back to my family in Miram Shah.

After this my younger brother, Gholam Moyahuddin, took up the jihad. In 1990, during the final days of the freedom movement, he took part in an attack upon the communist post of Darmalak village in the province of Khost. After a fierce battle the Soviets captured the area and we heard nothing from those who were taken prisoner. During his absence, I dreamed of my brother twice. The first time he appeared before me dressed in white and sat beside me on the bed. He told me that he had been wounded but that he was now recovered and able to return to us. It was this dream that kept our hopes alive.

An exchange of prisoners took place but my brother was not among them. By this time he had been away for many months. Then I had the second dream in which I came upon my brother in a field wearing a wreath of flowers on his head. When I tried to draw one of the flowers from the wreath, he told me that the wreath was a gift from Allah and that such favors were reserved for martyrs and could not be given away.

After the second dream we stopped looking for Gholam Moyahuddin. Allah had been telling me what had happened to my brother. Sixteen months later, when the Mujahedin recaptured the area from the Russians, my brother was found lying in the same spot where he had been killed all those months before. His body was as it had been on the day of battle. In time, he was brought to us here in Miram Shah and we gave him a proper martyr's burial.

Shamsuddin after being released from the hospital, 1987

Gholam Moyahuddin, brother of Shamsuddin, 1987

HAJI ABDUL

My father, Haji Gholam Sadiq, and five of my brothers were martyred during
the years of the jihad. It is a lucky family that offers the lives of their loved ones to
the cause of Allah. They have brought great blessings upon us. It was five years after
his death that I dreamed of my father. He sat at a great distance from me looking
away from where I stood. He was wearing a white turban and gazed off towards
the horizon. I asked him where he was. He turned to me and said that I should not
ask such questions, that I would meet him on the day of judgment.

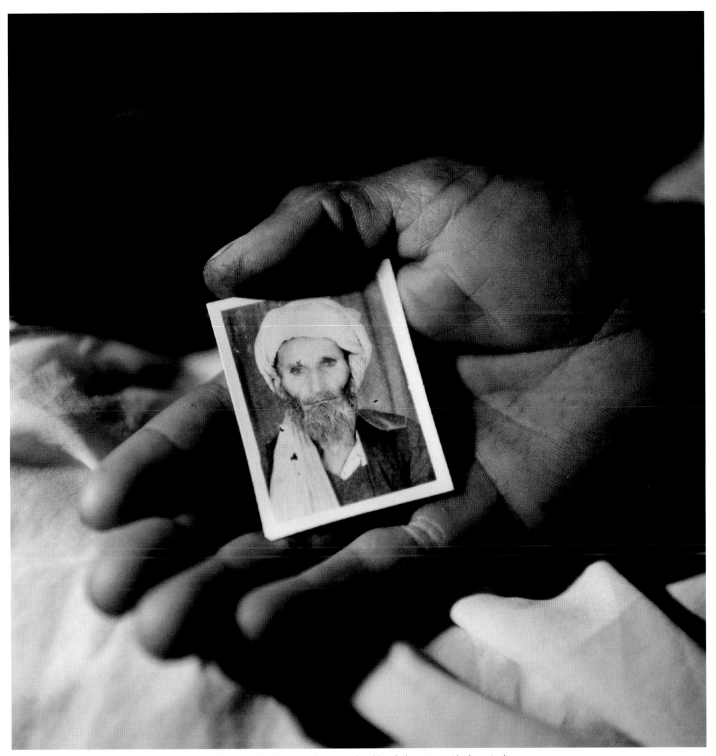

Haji Abdul holding a photograph of his father, Haji Gholam Sadiq

SAID ALI

My brother Abdul Abdi, son of Nasruddin, was only nineteen when he was martyred by a bombardment near the Jawara headquarters in 1988. He had been dead for four years when I dreamed of him. He was sitting beside a lamp. He told me that I should be patient, that the kindness of Allah will solve all our problems.

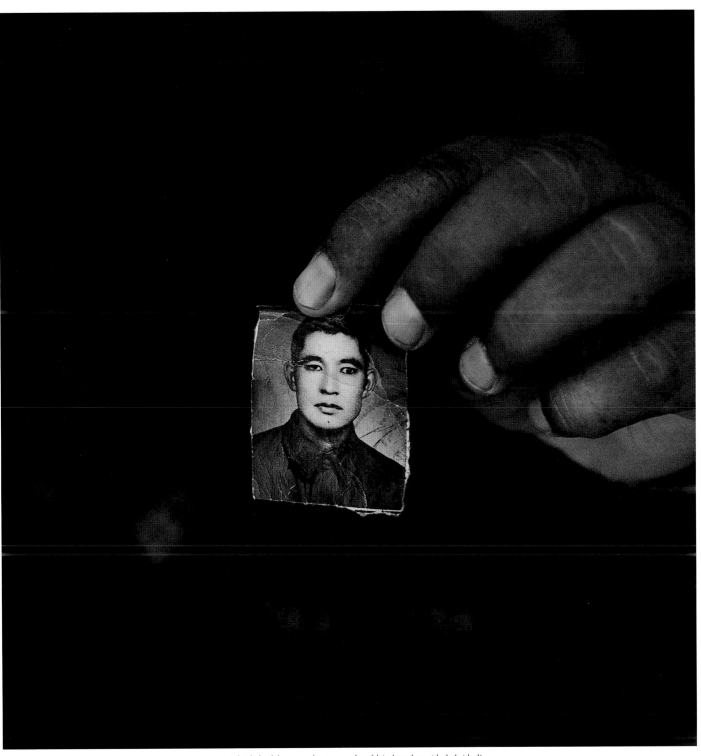

Said Ali holding a photograph of his brother Abdul Abdi

MOHAMMED YAQUB

The communists laid siege to our village for twelve days and nights. When the attack started I was some way from the village and able to make my way into the security of the mountains. My brother, Mohammed Azam, his two wives and their two children were not so lucky. They were caught and killed during the first day of the fighting. As the battle raged on there was no time to retrieve the bodies. For twelve days their bodies remained where they fell before we were able to return to the village and bury our dead. In my dreams I see Mohammed Azam walking among the fields. I approach him and ask him to return with me to our home. He tells me that he cannot. That his home is among the fields.

Abdul Aziz holding a photograph of his brother, Mula Abdul Hakim

TOUR JAN

My brother Bahauddin, son of Zarin, and my son, Sarfaraz, were martyred on the same day. My brother comes to me in my dreams and asks me to take care of his wife and four children.

Tour Jan holding a photograph of his brother, Bahauddin, and his son, Sarfaraz

HAJI QIAMUDDIN

My brother, Asamuddin, was killed in the 1988 battle for control of the Mazar-Kabul road. As I sleep, he walks in the streets of our home village with his Kalashnikov slung over his shoulder, just as he did when he was alive.

Haji Qiamuddin holding a photograph of his brother, Asamuddin

ABDULLAH

It was in 1986, the year of my twenty-eighth birthday, that I fought alongside my father, Sabz Ali, and my cousin, Abdul Ghafur, on the Zhawar front in Afghanistan. We were separated during the fighting and I felt that I was going to die. The only thing I could think of was my family. The communists captured the front and I fled along with the other surviving Mujahedin. When I realized that I would live, I knew that it was an extra blessing. I could stay with my family while bearing the blessings of a *ghazi*, a freedom fighter. I searched in vain for my father and cousin. Then I saw their bodies being carried by the other Mujahedin. Both of them had been killed during the battle. My cousin, who was only twenty-five years old at the time, had not even taken a wife.

When I visit my father in my dreams, I always see him alive. He advises me to do good and go to the mosque for prayer. We walk together in the fields without talking. We are together on the way.

Abdul Ghafur, cousin of Abdullah

No one need tell an orphan how to grieve.

Boy's burial mound

There is no light in the eyes of a childless man.

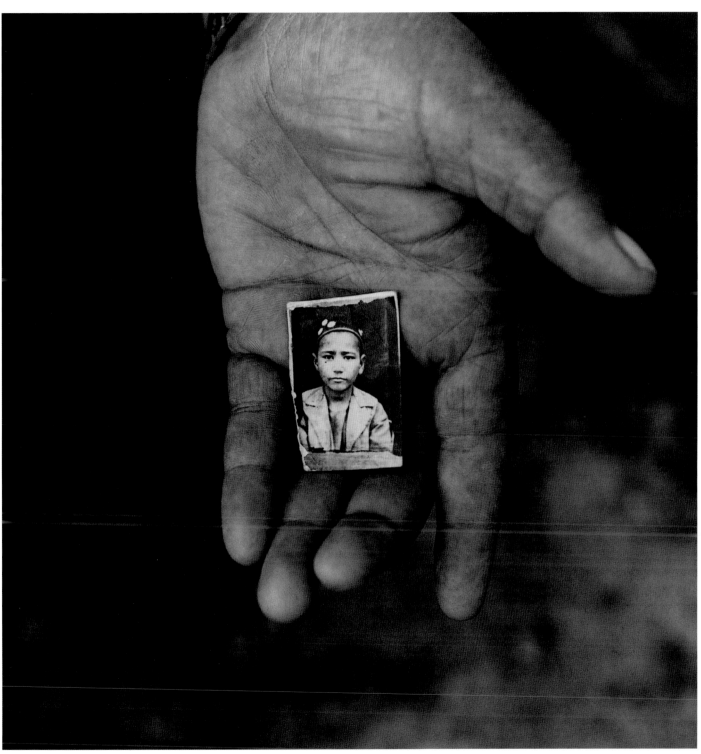

Child killed in Soviet bombardment

Hakim beside the grave of his sister; he cares for her three orphans

A WAKING DREAM

We had been guests for five days in the refugee village at Miram Shah in Pakistan. Following a night of discussion with the village elders, Abdul Sattar and I slept in the same room where they had gathered with their stories.

As the early morning call to prayer began, the men at my side stirred from their sleep and murmured to one another. They filed out into the dawn light to pay their respects to Allah, leaving me with the voice of the muezzin lingering in my ears.

It lured me back to another morning when I lay half-waking just before dawn, only days after my mother's sudden death. I remember peering up to the ceiling, checking the quality of the light as it began to make its trail across the room. I had just begun to realise that her loss would be with me for the rest of my life. That its legacy would change with time, but that the void it left behind would never be filled. Remembering that time, what came back to me with the greatest clarity and emotion was the dream I had that morning.

In my dream I was traveling down a long corridor, or some kind of ancient earthen passageway. As my gaze penetrated the depths I came upon myself. Approaching from behind, I realized it was not just my body, but rather, two bodies. As I entered myself, I felt that I was embracing, and being embraced by another.

I woke, still in the dream, with its force pulsating through my body. The second body, I came to realise, was my mother. In that dream, in that strange predawn hour had been a moment of empathy and mercy.

Holding this experience close to my heart, I heard refugees tell of missing brothers, sisters, sons and husbands. They remain in the dreams of the living.

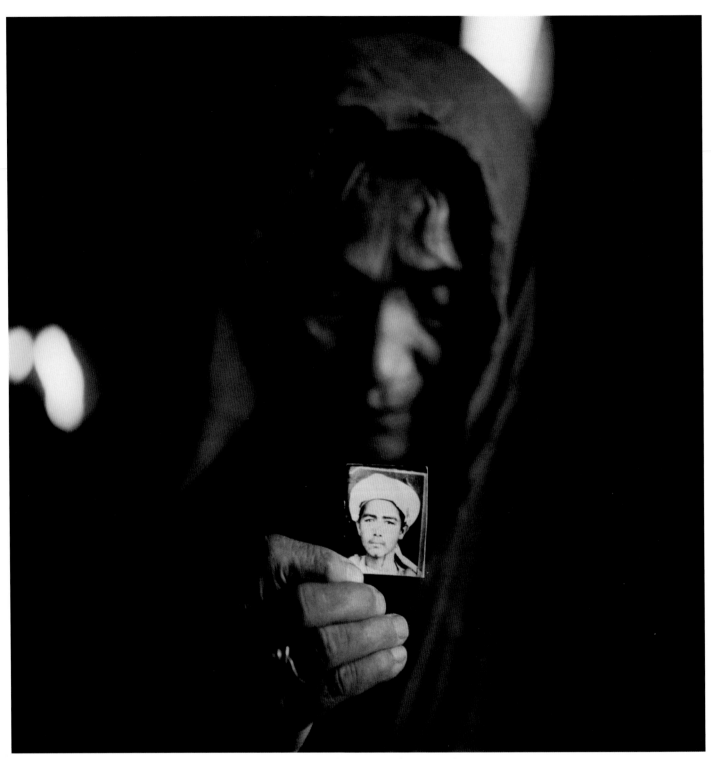

Qurban Gul holding a photograph of her son Mula Awaz

QURBAN GUL

Mula Awaz was my youngest son. In 1986, when he was eighteen years old, his group of Mujahedin attacked a communist post. In the exchange of fire, he was killed. Before the news of his death reached us, I dreamed that my son's body was being prepared for burial. When he had been washed and wrapped in white cloth, he was carried to the graveyard. They laid his body on the ground and turned his head towards Mecca. Then his body was covered with earth.

After that I did not dream of him again for several years. Then I became very ill and was taken to the hospital where I lay near death. Then I had the second dream of Mula Awaz. I was lying in my bed and I could hear the door to my hospital room opening. Mula Awaz appeared in the doorway and walked towards my bed. He had a scarf draped about his shoulders. As he approached, he took the cloth from his neck and offered it to me. He told me to wrap it about myself. Then without another word he turned away and disappeared into the corridor. I covered myself with the scarf and a sensation of warmth moved throughout my body. In the coming days, the illness left me and I was able to return home. I never dreamed of him again.

Qurban Gul

MAZARI

My husband died a long time before the coming of the communist troops. Our two sons were only children, and as they grew, I was the only one responsible for them. Without a father, it was my place to guide them in the world. They were teenagers when our country was invaded by the communists. For a short period we stayed in Afghanistan, then we fled with other villagers from our area to the refugee camp here at Miram Shah.

My oldest son, Abdul Malik, asked my permission to join the jihad. I knew that he was following the way of Allah and I allowed him to go. He traveled back into Afghanistan with the Mujahedin and I did not see him for months at a time, nor did we hear anything about him. It was only when he returned to Miram Shah with his group that we knew he was safe.

Then in 1987 there was an attack on the military post in our home village in Afghanistan. During that fighting, my son, Abdul Malik, was martyred with a bullet. His body was taken back to the village by the Mujahedin and he was buried in the lands surrounding our home. Two months later, the news of my son's death reached us here in Pakistan. When the family was told, Khail Mohammed, Abdul Malik's younger brother, vowed not to let his martyred brother's rifle rest.

One night I dreamt of Abdul Malik. He came to me and told me to bring him some water. I brought the water and he began to wash. Then he took off his shirt and showed me where he had been wounded in the back. On seeing the wound, I awoke. Two years later, my second son Khail Mohammed was also martyred by a shot from an anti-aircraft gun. We learned of his death three months after he had been killed. I dreamt of Khail Mohammed walking in a garden. He was surrounded by trees heavy with fruit. When I tried to enter the garden and go to him, I awoke.

Mazari

Abdul Malik, Mazari's first son, early 1980's

Khail Mohammed, Mazari's second son, early 1980's

BIBI MAH

Our village was a place of peace. The Mujahedin were not active in the region and we thought we would be safe from communist attacks. Then, without warning, the bombing started. We women could not leave our children so we stayed in our homes. In those early days we thought our homes were safe enough, but we soon began to understand the kind of destruction these weapons could bring. Many of our women and children were killed during this period.

The bombing continued and we were forced to leave. We walked to the Pakistani border, traveling at night to avoid the Soviets, and once our families were safely in Pakistan, the men returned on foot to our home village of Ibrahim Khel to take up the jihad.

My son, Haji Nour Ahmed, was among them. He and his group lived in our village and conducted their operations from there. When the communists came, they would escape to the safety of the mountains. Then, during one of these Russian operations, our village was surrounded. The Mujahedin escaped to the mountains as they had in the past. The Soviets, however, pretended to leave the area, but some of their forces stayed behind, waiting for the villagers to return. I was told that my son left the mountains early and was captured by the soldiers. They tortured him for information about the other Mujahedin and then martyred him with a bullet.

I have never learned to read but I was taught about the Koran and the Prophet Muhammad — peace be upon him — by the mullahs of our home village. Only with honesty in one's heart may a person claim their true reward. I was told that I need not understand every verse of the Koran to know that the religious way is to fight for one's faith. Heaven is a desert where everyone must make their own place. The families of the *shahid* are guaranteed a place.

I know that my son's death in the jihad has made him a *shahid*. He is blessed in heaven. Some day we will live there together. Now, when I visit him in my dreams, he sits in silence.

Bibi Mah

Abdul Shakour's eldest wife, Najiba

OUR PLIGHT

There has been much discussion about how Afghan women have been treated, how they have been abused, tortured and killed. But these discussions, which take place both inside and outside Afghanistan, have done little to solve our lack of basic human rights. Many Afghan women look to the West in the name of freedom and expect people in the West to promote our rights. But in the West they neither consult us about the issues that affect our daily lives, nor do they uphold or promote on our behalf the standards by which they themselves live.

History has taught us that a bright future is nothing but a mirage for Afghan women. The reality is tears, chained hands and silenced mouths. Afghan mothers who have brought up brave sons and husbands are generous, loving people but they have never succeeded in obtaining their independence. All our hopes have been consigned to the dustbin of history. Our voices have been buried without any recognition that our hands have carried swords to fight against our enemies.

Now we cover our heads with veils and slave like ants, carrying food to the mountains of Nuristan. In the north we are born to weave rugs, in the south to raise cattle and sheep and to clean the stables. Young girls are sold on markets like cattle and slaves — I don't mean in past centuries; the practice continues today.

We are often the casualties of ignorance. It is obvious from the beginning of our lives that we should only know how to eat, sleep, defecate, procreate and raise offspring to take our places. We have rarely known a life better than slavery. When the former Soviet Union occupied our country they sent our girls and women to Russia in the name of higher education. These women, who were indoctrinated and used for propaganda purposes, were not given any religious or secular rights, and they continued to be abused, often as a commodity for men. While a few found new freedoms after being released from our own country, others soon became disillusioned and eventually returned to their homeland in shame, or remained depressed in the former Soviet Union and former Eastern Bloc states.

When our great Islamic revolution succeeded, we thought our day of deliverance had come. Finally we would be free and independent. Afghanistan was released. But once again women were treated as the goat in the game, pulled this way and that by one faction or another. Once again, on all sides, indiscriminate bombing and rocket-attacks, bullets and mines killed Afghan children in their mother's wombs. We were forced to flee with bare feet and uncovered heads to escape the killing. Some of us fled to foreign countries and became refugees. It should not be forgotten that some of us were forced to flee to Moscow for our safety!

I shall never forget how so many of us spent frightened lonely nights waiting patiently in the front line for a single loaf of bread. How many of us were abducted by armed men from Mujahedin parties in the middle of the day in busy streets. How many of us were raped. How many of us threw themselves from buildings to keep their chastity. How many of us were taken from the scorching refugee camps in Jalalabad to become a commodity for men in neighboring countries. How many widows were forced to sell themselves to feed their families.

Those who have come to power, those with guns, continue to leer at us, to make fun of us, to take pleasure in harassing us. These men who think of themselves as the defenders of our faith, as our fathers and brothers sent to protect us, are the same ones who call us "Honey". They say: "Don't come out of your bottle, the flies might touch you." The flies are the men that rush at you. Others tell us that we are "live wires that must be covered." It is a pity they don't recognize us as individuals, as fellow human beings. Over the loudspeakers they announce that fourteen years of holy war has simply been to cover Afghan women in Muslim dress.

That, dear brother, dear father and son, I am sure was not the purpose of the holy war. What you have brought is corruption, blasphemy and destruction. When those "sincere, truthful freedom fighters" entered Kabul they married young women by force. But no one was willing to marry a widow to change her tragic life. Sisters, it does not matter to the leaders and commanders who claim to be supporters of the Afghan nation that you may be killed by shrapnel fired by our Muslim brothers. It makes no difference to them that you don't have fuel for your lamps and spend nights in the dark while they watch satellite television.

We were not born to decorate ourselves with ornaments. Our prized possessions are pens and books. We are plunging into an abyss of adversity, and neither our role in society nor our potential have ever been recognized. All we can try to do is move forward towards our freedom. There is no magic wand that will give it to us instantly. We have been ignored by our own fathers, brothers and sons, and abandoned by our sisters from outside our country who have fought and won their own freedoms after many long and painful battles. We must wake up and make something of ourselves. We have a responsibility and duty to our offspring. How much longer must we wait? We have waited long enough. It is time to improve our lot in life and throw off the shackles that have allowed the caravan of civilization and democracy to travel far beyond us.

Letter written by a woman forced to flee to exile in Pakistan — 1998

AAKILA

I lived with my parents and six brothers and sisters in the Makrorian section of Kabul near the Dostum militia. My father, Asil Khan, was a chemistry teacher. I was very young when he had his accident. In 1992 he was walking towards the old part of Makrorian and as he came to the bridge he stepped on an anti-personnel mine. Neighbors took him to the Charsad Besdar (four-hundred-bed) hospital where they amputated his right leg and right hand.

There was a great deal of rocket fire and one morning in 1994 the heavy fighting came to our area. After a week there was a lull and my family got the chance to flee. We traveled to the camp at Jalalabad where we lived for a time. Then last year my mother became very ill. They told us that she had hepatitis. A week later she was dead and from that time I became responsible for the family. With my six brothers and sisters, Salim, Masoum, Kamila, Matin, Adeila, and Samim, my father and I traveled south to Pakistan hoping to find a better situation. When we first arrived he was forced to spend our savings and then we were given a ration pass. My father began washing sand for money.

My father says that if there is peace, then we can think about improving our lives. But if there is war, then we have no chance. Everything will be drained by the fighting effort. The people of Afghanistan cannot think of their homes. Those who are fighting are thinking of their own interests and their power. He says that it will not change soon.

Aakila

Asil Khan, Aakila's father

Salim, Aakila's brother

SHAH PARAY

I had ten children. We heard that Pakistan would be a clean place and a safe haven from the war and the whole family migrated there more than a year ago. For the first three months we remained in the refugee camp without any money. My two boys, Javed and Janshid, were the eldest. During this period I was trying to get work, but there was none to be found. At the end of Ramadhan our neighbor came and told me that he would take my two sons to the brick factories for work. We trusted him. We thought he would protect our boys. At the time they were sixteen and seventeen years old. We had no money and finally we took the decision to send them away with our neighbor. We had no news about them for three months. Then we received a letter from them saying that they had been sold. It seemed that the boys had asked for their pay at the brick factory and had been told that they had no right to ask for money as they had been sold to the owner by our Afghan neighbor.

They were in an unfamiliar part of Pakistan and it had been impossible for them to escape. They could not speak the language and had no money with which to travel. They were completely lost. After some weeks, the boys met a refugee in the factory who was from the camp. He was a trader and often traveled to remote areas to try and sell used clothes. When the boys heard that he was from our village, they asked him to bring us back a letter.

After discussions with the elders, we decided that the best thing for us to do was to send the trader back to the village in an attempt to free our boys. He went with a group of men and received the boys in the middle of the night. They sneaked away from the village and made it back to the camp without incident. Our neighbor never returned.

KUKUGUL

Many people left our country during the revolution. My husband was named Mohammed Usman and I was the elder of his two wives. Between us two mothers we had eleven children and we lived in the Rahman Mina area of Kabul. Ours was a village of some two hundred families.

My husband was a road construction worker in the Parwan section of Kabul. In 1985 his car was hit by a rocket while he was working for the government. The Mujahedin attacked him because it was a government vehicle. After his death the communists gave us a house and a government pension. We didn't know where else to go, so we stayed in Kabul in the hope that the children could finish their schooling.

Then in 1992 the heavy fighting between the Mujahedin factions began. By 1994 most of the children had finished their schooling and the situation in the streets grew worse. One night I was sleeping in my house when a rocket came suddenly from out of nowhere. It was a big rocket like a Sacher 20 and it left a deep hole inside the house and the yard. My bed was completely destroyed, but miraculously I was saved, though I was badly injured. The rest of the family was at a wedding celebration so they escaped. It was lucky I was at home alone.

I had many shrapnel wounds and some of the Mujahedin from my neighborhood took me to the ICRC hospital. Since that was in the area of the Hazaras and I was Sunni, we were soon shifted to Kabul city hospital where there was greater safety. Later, my son-in-law brought me to Pakistan to join the rest of the family. Since then our home has been destroyed and looted by the Dostum militia.

Allah knows better who has brought the fighting to Afghanistan and caused its people to live in destruction. I am not a journalist, but I am able to speak out about the war and its effects on the community. I would like to return to my country, but I know this war has brought devastation. When peace, education and facilities are in place, then I will be prepared to go home. The bird sings sad songs, even in a golden cage.

Kukugul's husband, Mohammed Usman, early 1980's

ROHGUL

I was married to a police officer and we had a very good life together in Afghanistan. We were blessed with five children and a home in the beautiful Demaizang area of Kabul. One day in 1989 my husband was shot on his way home from work by one of the Mujahedin factions. He died immediately. The whole family was in a state of shock. After his death we had nowhere else to go so we had to stay in our home. I tried to keep up the hope that peace would return to our land but it was not to be. My neighborhood became the front line between two Mujahedin factions, the Hazaras and Gulbuddin's forces. The fighting increased in the streets until one day in 1992 a rocket landed in the courtyard of my own home. My youngest son Fawad was killed instantly and I was badly wounded. My neighbors took my other children and Fawad's body to my mother's house.

I was taken with the others who had been wounded in the blast to the hospital in Jalalabad. They told me that they were going to amputate my leg, but I became completely hysterical and refused to allow them to do it. I would not let them take my leg. So I was transferred to the Afghan training center, and though I had to remain in that hospital for many months, I was fortunate in the end to keep my leg. I was further blessed since a Pakistani shopkeeper looked after my children for three months until my cousin came and took them to stay with him in Hyatabad. When I was finally let out of the hospital I traveled south to Pakistan to live with my cousin. The shopkeeper helped me to get a ration pass and a tent in the refugee village at Nasir Bagh. In those days it was very difficult to be registered as a refugee and he helped me out of the kindness of his heart.

In Nasir Bagh we were soon moved to a house and my eldest son Farid began to contribute to our home. He was only twelve years old and working in a hotel in Peshawar. Last year there was a strike at the hotel and the workers were attacked. In the fighting a pot of boiling milk was dropped on Farid and he was severely scalded. He was in the hospital for five days and eventually he died from his wounds.

I miss my country so terribly. I am homesick all the time. I have seen hundreds of people die in this war. Once I saw the Hazaras kill more than seventy people at once at the Russian cultural center. They massacred them as they were leaving work for the day. I have been told that my home has been completely destroyed in the civil war, but I still hold on to the hope that there will be a time when I can return to the land where I was born. I will return when the government gives its people jobs rather than Kalashnikovs.

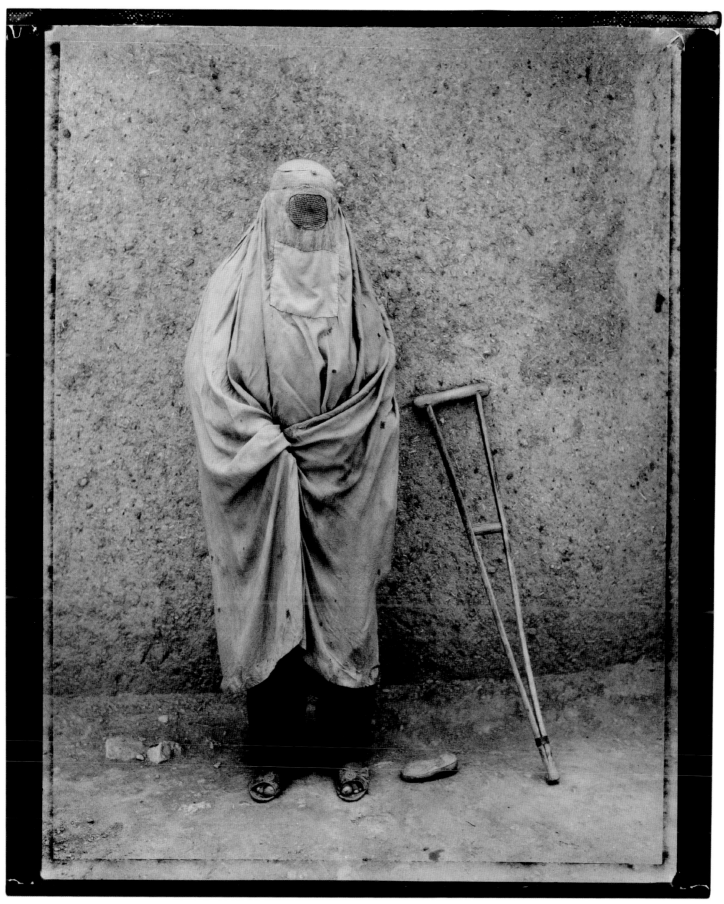

Rohgul

Rohgul

RABIA

I was at home with my cousins and the ground began to move. We thought it was
an earthquake, and ran out of the house but soon we realized that it was Shi'is
and Hazaras who had been digging a tunnel under the house. They came out and
surrounded our family but luckily our neighbor was also Hazara and he told
the men that we were Hazaras and not to hurt us. They let us go. That neighbor
saved our lives.

On the same day they kidnapped another neighbor's wife and took her back
to their base. After a few days they came back to tell the husband he could come
and collect his wife. When he got to their base they brought his wife before him
naked and asked her to dance. When she refused she was told that they would kill
her husband if she did not perform. The husband tried to grab one of the weapons
from the Hazaras to kill himself, but they stopped him and took him back to his
house. He told the story to his mother, and then he died. His heart had been broken.

Some days later they brought his wife back to the house. She was already
dead. Her breasts were cut and she had no eyes. I attended the funeral service and
saw for myself. Any woman who survives such an assault or who escaped would
commit suicide. They never come back. The shame of confronting their families and
husbands would be too much to bear. Under these conditions, it is better not to
remain alive. In the days following this event we decided to leave our home and
flee to Pakistan.

Pakistani Secret Police

Cousins

Khalid

Osman and Farid, blind *qari,* "one who knows the Koran by heart", brothers

JOURNEY TO AFGHANISTAN

In the winter of 1997, Abdul Sattar and I made a trip from Peshawar in the north-western corner of Pakistan to the Afghan capital of Kabul. I had last been there in August the previous year, just a month before the Taliban took over the city, and for a few weeks afterward the world's media had focused attention on the new regime of "Islamic fundamentalists", particularly their acts of repression against women. While we were in Pakistan, UNHCR reports (United Nations High Commissioner for Refugees) had kept me posted about the political climate inside the country, where the Taliban had imposed their version of Sheria law. After months spent listening to the refugees' stories of how they had been forced to leave their country, I wanted to go back into Afghanistan and to see the changes to Kabul with my own eyes. As I traveled with Abdul Sattar, their stories provided me with a structure and rhythm for the way I engaged with the country.

Our journey followed the route of the refugee exodus in reverse; the journey that the Afghans living in exile were unable to make. Already one generation has died in exile in the border villages of Pakistan, and from their graveyards, standing among the burial mounds, it is possible to look out across the land to the mountains inside Afghanistan.

The physical passage from Peshawar to Kabul is a journey through the history of the Afghan nation. In the tribal regions of north-western Pakistan, there is the feel of a feudal kingdom where abandoned citadels cresting the ridges are reminders of Britain's attempted conquest in the last century. The desert and the rolling foothills are scarred by two decades of Soviet bombing and oppression. The high mountain ranges provide a respite from the ravages of human history, before the edge of the Kabul plateau marks the beginning of the sprawling ruined suburbs which were the battleground of small determined bands of Mujahedin during the civil war. In the industrial hinterland, derelict factories have been gutted by looting Mujahedin factions, and in the city center itself crossed by innumerable invisible front lines, a new chapter of Afghan history is unfolding.

Abdul Sattar arrived at my room just after the morning prayer and we made our way toward the bus depot where we were pointed to a van destined for the Afghan border. While we waited for it to fill up hawkers milled around with eggs, hot *naans*, bread, cigarettes and chewing gum. It was the sugar-cane season and the rhythmic clank of the slicing machine reverberated in the distance.

When the van had been successfully packed with travelers we lurched forward through the bazaar, jockeying for position with rickshaws and bicycles, crawling along narrow byways in a blare of horns, squeezing past buses decorated with mirrors and ornate gilded paintings of Indian movie stars. Defeated traffic police stood at the side of the road and pedestrians disappeared in clouds of exhaust as we left the bazaar behind and the road opened on to the highway to Afghanistan.

Peshawar borders the Khyber Tribal Agency, one of the autonomous regions along Pakistan's northern frontier. The Pathans who live in the area take great pride in their tradition of defiance, and are allowed their independence as historically they have fought to keep invading armies from sweeping south into Pakistan. The highway through this region had been closed intermittently due to flare-ups of ancient blood feuds. After the border check, the transition into the Tribal Agency was marked by storefronts bursting with weapons of all descriptions and men armed with handguns and Kalashnikovs. I thought of a story Abdul Sattar had told me about a Pathan villager who received a man into his home and during their conversation had asked him to stay for the evening meal. The visitor demurred, but as was the custom, the Pathan villager asked him again. Once more the man refused. The host asked for a third time, and when the visitor again refused, the host accepted that the man had already eaten and was satisfied. They continued to talk for some time before the visitor left. Later while passing a neighbor's house, the host heard the voice of the man who had just visited him. Peering through the window, he saw the visitor sitting with his neighbor eating the evening meal. He wondered what his neighbor must think of a man who accepts a guest into his home without the hospitality of a shared meal. He was gripped by such humiliation that he ran home, returned with a Kalashnikov and shot the guest dead.

It was not the first time that Abdul Sattar had explained the rituals of hospitality to me. During our travels together, I was often confounded by the narrow line dividing generosity from the codes of honor and revenge. On one of our first trips to the village of Ghazi in Pakistan we had passed some bee-keepers who were gingerly plucking combs of honey from the hives. Covered in bees and honey, one of the workers recognized Abdul Sattar and waved for us to stop. As we got out of the car the men abandoned their work and ran to embrace us. Greetings and jokes were followed by an invitation to see them at work. We were led to the machine which extracts honey from its comb. The honeycomb is placed in a rotating cylinder which holds back the waxy shell while the nectar is thrust to the sides and drips into a vat. After the demonstration, the keepers produced two weighty jars of honey for Abdul Sattar. He protested for several minutes, but ultimately accepted the gift as the bee-keepers beamed with joy. Driving away he explained that to refuse their offer would have implied that he was, in some way, better than them, that he pitied them. By accepting the gift, he allowed them a sense of pride which far exceeded the satisfaction of a few rupees.

In the foothills leading to the Khyber Pass where the barren British fortresses rise on the horizon, we met bicycle smugglers heading back across the border with their double-bike charges. Riding one bike with the second strapped on behind, they approached each small hillside pedaling laboriously, then dismounted and slogged to the top before cruising down and repeating the whole sequence again until the last furious descent into Pakistan. The landscape was dotted with circular stone dwellings clinging to the hillside. Occasionally children bolted from their homes to gawk at our passing vehicle with its cautious driver eyeing the precipice at the unguarded side of the road. In the heart of the Tribal Agency, we rounded a bend and came across an enormous mansion, its walls stretching skywards. The splendor of the building seemed out of place, but Abdul Sattar told me it had been the home of the drug runner Haji Ayub. Afghanistan supplies seventy per cent of the world's heroin and Haji Ayub was one of its main traffickers. For years he operated from the security of his palace in the Tribal Agency. Then, by some strange twist of events, Haji Ayub traveled to New York and surrendered to the United States Drug Enforcement Agency. Apparently, he believed surrendering to the authorities, whom he had evaded for years, warranted a reward of leniency. This colossal miscalculation led to his imprisonment in America while his abandoned fortress in the Khyber Pass posts an ominous threat to those tempted to follow its owner's path.

As the mountains opened on to the high plateau our eyes ranged freely to the horizon, which was broken by a group of Kuchi nomads wending their way through the barren landscape beside camels carrying their belongings. With their chiseled features and brilliantly colored dress, these people claim their place in the vast expanse and challenge its supremacy. Traditionally, they roamed throughout Afghanistan, living on the plains in winter and moving into the mountains to escape the summer heat. But in the past two decades their nomadic culture has been threatened as scores of tribal members and their herds have been killed by land-mines. The Kuchis, oblivious to the war and yet the victims of it, have suffered some of the greatest human cost of the conflict.

The heart of the desert lies just before Jalalabad, the first town en route from Pakistan to Kabul. Small mud-brick houses lined the sides of the road, sanctuaries from the blasts of heat and cold that alternately assault the area. As we drove through in January, winter had swept through the landscape, numbing its inhabitants. But it was in this inhospitable terrain that Sar Shahi, the first camp for internally displaced people, was erected in 1994. Soon it was home to thousands of Afghans seeking refuge from the turmoil in the north of the country who remained here, at the mercy of the climate, refusing to allow the war to banish their resolve.

Many of the refugees I met in Pakistan had spent time in this camp. Aakila, whose name means "wise", was here when her mother died of hepatitis. In Sar Shahi she was forced to change from an eight-year-old girl into a woman with responsibility for an entire household before fleeing with her disabled father and five young brothers and sisters to Pakistan. I had been to the camp in July 1996 during a time of heavy fighting between Mujahedin factions battling for control of the region. The lack of security meant that travel to the camp was only permitted with an armed escort. In the mornings we would join the UNHCR team as they drove to the camp along a road shimmering in the distance. While they addressed the crowds gathered outside the UNHCR office we walked through the camp.

One morning a man named Gul Ajan, who lived with his family in the camp, invited us to share the midday meal. Again, in keeping with the protocol in Afghan communities, such a request for our company made only twice would have allowed Gul Ajan to retain his dignity without actually warranting an acceptance. However, he requested our company three times, implying the offer was genuine and we agreed to return for the meal. When we arrived, our host was standing outside his home. He wore a desert-softened gray *silvar*, the traditional Afghan knee-length shirt and trousers, and the white turban draped about his shoulders mingled with rivulets of hair and beard. We entered the compound where his children unfurled a carpet beneath an open-air tent. Gul Ajan invited us to sit in the shade on the richly patterned rug and motioned to one of the children who disappeared into the family quarters returning moments later with a tray of food which he placed beside his father. With quiet precision, Gul Ajan drew the bowls across the rug towards his guests. As is Afghan tradition, the first dishes with the largest and choicest portions were given to the visitors and the last to the family. We sat cross-legged together, sharing their meal of yogurt, *naans*, eggs, and green tea.

While we ate, one of Gul Ajan's children knelt by my side furiously fanning the meal to keep the flies at bay and a pet Mynah bird danced from shoulder to shoulder looking for the best position from which to swoop down for a snack. In conversation which ranged from his family to our journey and the situation in Jalalabad, Gul Ajan spoke of the difficulty of life in the camp and his belief that his family would return to their northern village when the fighting ended. Each hopeful statement about the end of war and a return home was followed by the declaration, "Insha'allah", if Allah wills. When we had eaten our fill, Gul Ajan pleaded with us to take more, claiming that we had not eaten enough to be satisfied. We took a few small bites to please our host before he led us in a prayer of thanks. We followed him in raising our hands as if reading from an imaginary book while reciting the verses. At the close of the prayer we brought our hands before our faces and then beside our heads to envelop ourselves in the final words of the prayer: "Alhamdu li'llah," praise be to Allah. Then we stood up, bidding our host "Khoda hafiz," Allah protect you, and stepped out from the shade into the blazing afternoon.

Now, looking out of the van many months later, I still expected to see Gul Ajan at the entrance to his home, his broad smile animating his face as it had on the day we met him. But in the time between, UNHCR assistance had been withdrawn and the residents forced to move on. The camp had been abandoned and the tent of the open compound where we shared tea with our host lay in tatters.

Abdul Aziz

Binafshah and Naizgul

Sultan Skhinder and his son Spengar

Doctor Jan's son and friend

Mohammed Nawab and his nephew

Bai Murad Shah's daughter, Ziarrahman

Salim

Abdul Ghafur's daughter Zermina

Ghulam Dastiger

Hakimtullah, born in 1979, the year his family arrived in Pakistan

Afghan fighting dog

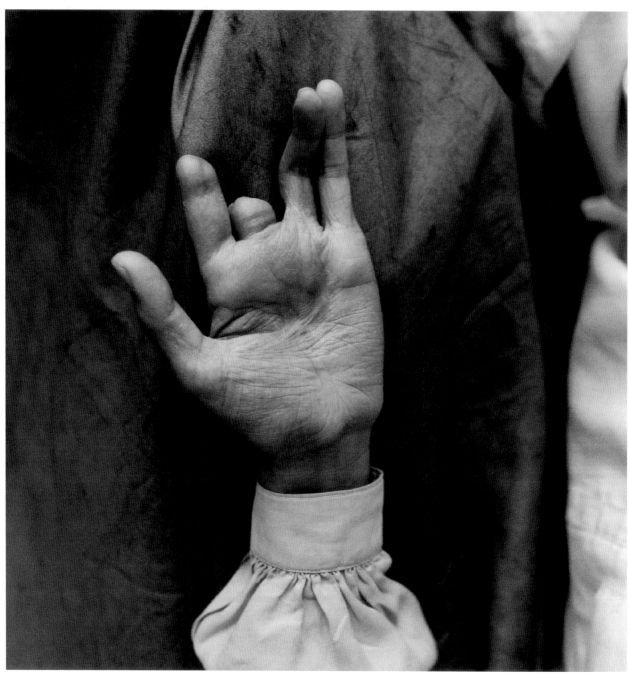

Mohammed Daud's hand, one year after picking up a butterfly mine he thought was a toy

Mohammed Daud

Andar

170

Abdullah

Molko and his brother Qaderkhan

THE STUDIO

The road to Jalalabad was strewn with the rusted carcasses of overturned tanks, grim symbols of the decades of occupation and civil war. As the first Taliban checkpost loomed up before us, we could see a group of young Taliban soldiers gathered in front of a makeshift barrier whose upright supports had thousands of tangled feet of audio tape, confiscated on earlier searches, wound around them, fluttering like ribbons in the wind. Each Talib wore a black turban, a *silvar*, and a Kalashnikov. Those standing at the roadside attended to passing vehicles while others sat on stools and discarded bed frames in the shade of a tree.

They motioned us to the side of the road. This was my first official encounter with the Taliban inside Afghanistan — I was traveling as an Afghan, since I was unsure what sort of response that would provoke if I was discovered to be a foreigner, dressed in a *silvar* with an Afghan hat and a *petou*, an Afghan blanket, draped around my shoulders. Though I had grown a beard, it was still not of the length prescribed by Sheria law, which dictates that when the beard is held in the fist beneath the chin, whiskers should protrude from the base of the hand. Violators were beaten with iron rods and imprisoned for the time it took to grow one of a suitable size. When the van came to a halt before the young Talib and as he strode towards the door, I rearranged my *petou*, tossing the cloth high over the shoulder to cover the lower part of my face. He bent to search beneath the seats for hidden weapons or smuggled goods while another probed the underside of the van. Satisfied with his search, the first Talib rose and stared hard into the face of each passenger. As he looked into my eyes, I returned his gaze and realized they were the eyes of a young man, a boy almost, who could be no more than fifteen years old. His eyes dismissed mine and moved toward those of the passenger by my side. Without having uttered a word, he slid the door closed and waved us on.

On the tree-lined stretch of road leading to Jalalabad, Abdul Sattar pointed toward the mountains of the Hindu Kush towering in the distance. Laghman, his family home, was only thirty kilometers away, but the risk of being detained in such a remote area had been too great to allow us to travel that way. The aroma of burning wood mixing with dust and the blare of early evening traffic signaled our arrival in the town. While Abdul Sattar visited the mosque to offer prayer, I sat at a *chaikhane*, a tea house, sipping green tea which grew more bitter cup by cup as the lump of sugar dissolved. From where I sat I could see the mosque across the street with the sun setting beyond the minaret and hear the people in the bazaar bargaining for household goods on their way home. Behind the shops in the money changers' alley, men sat engulfed by piles of cash, seemingly oblivious to the possibility of theft. Travelers like us, recently arrived from Pakistan, were walking along in search of the best exchange rate: a few Pakistani rupees for a stack of Afghanis.

The voice of the muezzin rose above the commotion calling the citizens to prayer. An old man, unable to leave his goods, stood on top of the table that doubled as his stall and made himself ready in the middle of the bazaar. He drew a rag from around his shoulders and arranged it on the table top with respectful precision, transforming the spot into holy ground. As pedestrians scurried past, he shut his eyes whispering "Bismi 'llah," in the name of Allah, while passing his arms beside his ears then before his chest. He recited the words softly while prostrating himself and placing his head down to rest upon the sacred rag. When he finished his prayer, he climbed down from his perch and his young son climbed up. In duplicating his father's movements, the boy seemed transformed into a man.

Abdul Sattar joined me and we sat together finishing the tea and taking in the bazaar as the night market grew busy under the radiance of hissing gaslamps. I had first met Abdul Sattar in Peshawar, when I was beginning to visit the Afghan villages and needed an interpreter, and over the past two years he had given me a rare opportunity for insight into Afghanistan. At forty-three, he had lived through the political upheavals in his country and understood the complexities and contradictions inherent to the culture. He had graduated from Kabul University before bringing his family to Pakistan in the early days of Soviet occupation. He, and the other elders of his village established the Afghan refugee community of Ghazi. Since then, he had been the principal of a *madrasa*, a religious school, as well as an employee of various relief agencies.

Like so many others, Abdul Sattar had fought against the Soviets with the conviction that the jihad would bring a glorious future to the people under an Islamic state. He told me, when the Soviets withdrew, he had shared first the pride in the Mujahedin victory and then the bitter disappointment as the commanders abandoned the cause of Allah and pursued their own interests. The jihad lost its meaning for him and he returned to Pakistan with the realization that the triumph of the Mujahedin was only a pause in the war-making.

During our travels, I was with him when he prayed five times a day. On road trips he planned his day carefully, offering a longer prayer at midday leaving the afternoon free for travel. If we were in a group, a prayer mat was placed in the middle of the room and Abdul Sattar performed his *nemaz* in the midst of the gathering. Men came and went, changing their steps so as not to cross the path to Allah. He sat with palms outstretched and legs folded beneath him on the rug, his face softening into an expression I only saw during prayer. His lips moved as muffled incantations broke the silence. From time to time he would open his eyes with a gaze fixed upon a place that left me far behind.

In public, I had learned to be cautious when discussing Islam for fear of being misinterpreted, but with Abdul Sattar I spoke openly. Once I asked why he allowed me such latitude in our talks and he answered that he felt my heart was right and my inquiry genuine. He said that the nature of Islam was not defensive and that it welcomed questioning when the motives were pure because through such probing the inherent truth of the religion would be revealed.

When I told Abdul Sattar that I did not fully understand the nature of the jihad, he offered me a parable about Hazrat Ali from the Hadith, the Islamic principles. During the jihad, Hazrat Ali was in hand-to-hand combat with an infidel. Having gained the advantage, he sat astride the infidel with his sword to his throat. When Hazrat Ali asked the man to convert to Islam, the infidel spat in his face. At that moment, instead of killing him, Hazrat Ali took the sword from the infidel's throat and set him free. Shocked by the act, the infidel asked Hazrat Ali why he had not killed him. Hazrat Ali said that if he had killed the infidel at that moment, it would have been to release his own anger — a personal act of revenge — and therefore not in the name of Allah and the spirit of the jihad. The infidel was so taken with the purity of Hazrat Ali's insight that he converted to Islam.

Abdul Sattar explained how the significance of prayer was not often understood within the Afghan communities. In the *madrasas,* religious texts are instilled in students through repetition. In a country where less than one per cent of the people are literate, the average Afghan prays to fulfill his religious duty without understanding the meaning of the words he recites. The act alone satisfies the societal demand for respectful prayer. But without understanding, the offering of prayer is stripped of its essence and devoid of the ability to guide and nurture the soul.

When we moved inside to order dinner, the gravelly voice of a Taliban mullah loomed in the background. He sang in praise of Allah and the coming of the Taliban to Afghanistan. He described them alternately as saviors, defending the people from the threat of the infidels, and builders of the true Islamic state with Sheria law for all Muslims. I knew that before our arrival in Jalalabad the Taliban officers of conduct had been despatched to tour the city in preparation for the visit of a Taliban minister from Kabul, and that many of the townspeople had been beaten and detained for actions that the Taliban deemed contrary to Sheria law.

We ate in silence for several minutes, listening to the mullah's drone. Suddenly, as though he were apologizing for the entire society, Abdul Sattar said: "The problem is not with Islam, it is with the Muslims themselves. If everyone acted by the word of Allah, then we would have the best, most peaceful society. But these people are selfish, they are acting with their own interests at heart. If the people to whom the mullahs are preaching are not able to read, they must rely upon the word of those who are learned. A great responsibility rests with those men. Sometimes it happens that they misuse their power."

I asked Abdul Sattar more about the Taliban. I knew that he had shared the early optimism of the refugees in Pakistan for what the Taliban might do for Afghanistan. He told me that twice they had sent emissaries to his home in Jalalabad asking that he play a role in the new government. When they came for a third time, he knew that he would have to accept and traveled to Kabul to take up his appointment. He recounted weeks spent in an empty office without responsibility while key ministerial positions were given to young Mujahedin commanders who controlled the city neighborhoods and surrounding countryside. He said that these men were neither devout Muslims nor capable of fulfilling their ministerial duties. One day, after months spent waiting patiently for the development of some policy he could follow, he walked out of his office and returned to exile in Pakistan.

Later, when we had finished our dinner and were walking through the streets of the town, we passed a fruitseller's stall, its bright lights illuminating the brilliant reds and yellows of the apples and persimmons, apricots and pomegranates, and casting a faint light on the facade of the closed shop next door. Above it a sign in ornate lettering read "Maiwand Photo Studio", and through the window I could just make out a scattering of discarded picture frames with their insides ripped out lying on the ground and strewn about the bottom of a display case. Maiwand is the area around Kandahar through which the British made their initial incursion into Afghanistan. During the battle of Maiwand the Afghans sustained many casualties before winning a victory against the British and forcing them to retreat. The name was invoked as a source of national pride in the decades that followed.

We knocked on the door and entered a tiny room where the outlines of missing images haunted the dusty walls. In the dim light of a candle, the man behind the desk introduced himself as Ridzwanul Haq. He embraced us and welcomed us to his studio. He told us that in the first days of their rule, the Taliban claimed that a photograph or moving picture made of a living creature was akin to the creation of an idol, and according to Sheria must be outlawed. By closing cinemas and destroying representations of living beings, the Taliban removed any competition for the attention that was due to Allah. Ridzwanul Haq told us he saw photography as a service to the people. He wanted his sitters to look good so they would remember the time in their lives when the photograph was taken.

I told him that I was working on a book in which I hoped to be able to bring the voices of Afghans into other countries in the world. He smiled and said that if I brought such a book back to Afghanistan, it would be burned and I would be beaten and perhaps imprisoned. I asked him about the loss of his business and he shrugged: he had lived through many changes in government and believed it would only be a matter of time before his doors were open again.

In the moments before we left, he turned to the negatives lying in the bottom of the display case and said he was willing to let me use them in my book. I understood this as his act of defiance against the rule of the Taliban. He bent down, gathered the scarred and dusty negatives, and packed them in a box and handed them to me. With the box under my arm we bade him *Khoda hafiz* and stepped back into the bazaar. It was quiet now, and as we meandered through the streets the headlights of passing rickshaws cast our shadows on the road while the constellations in a moonless sky broke the black night.

On the first night of our return to Afghanistan, Abdul Sattar taught me the opening prayer before sleep. He told me that, because he cared for me as a brother, he wanted me to share the glory and wonder he found in Islam. I worried about the propriety of learning it, yet I followed the verses, my tongue struggling with the new shapes. As I repeated the words aloud, sending them into the night air, they felt strange and foreign, a borrowed grace. Later, when Abdul Sattar slept, I took out the box of negatives from the studio and began to sift through them. I held the images up one by one to the lamp beside my bed where they were animated by the glow. In the silent darkness it was as if I was meeting each person for the first time. There was one photograph of a woman. In the shadow of the box the veil betrayed her gender. Holding the negative between my thumb and index finger, I moved her towards the light. Her posture and the carriage of her head were resolute. Her eyes pierced the gap separating us. She held my gaze with the intensity of her own for several seconds before, breaking contact, I lay the image back in the box, closed the lid and snuffed out the light.

Studio photographs from Jalalabad (pages 179–190)

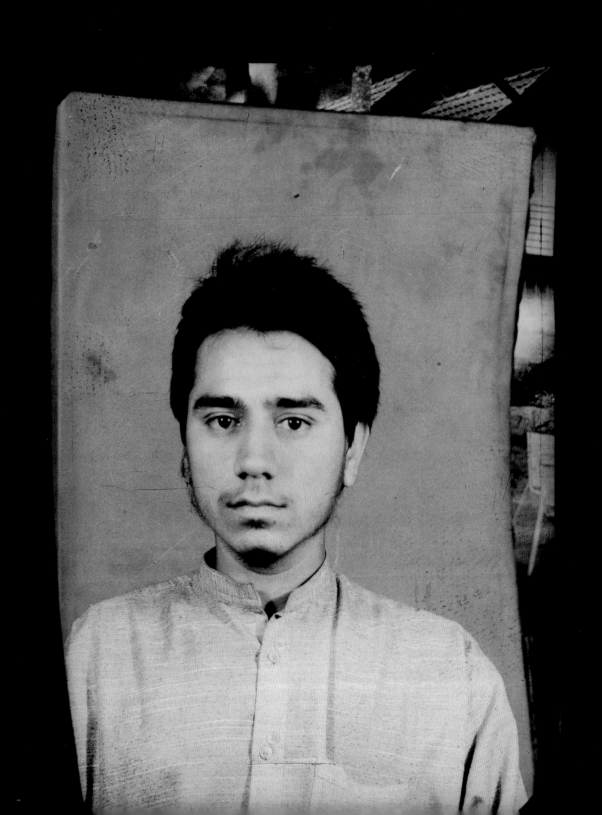

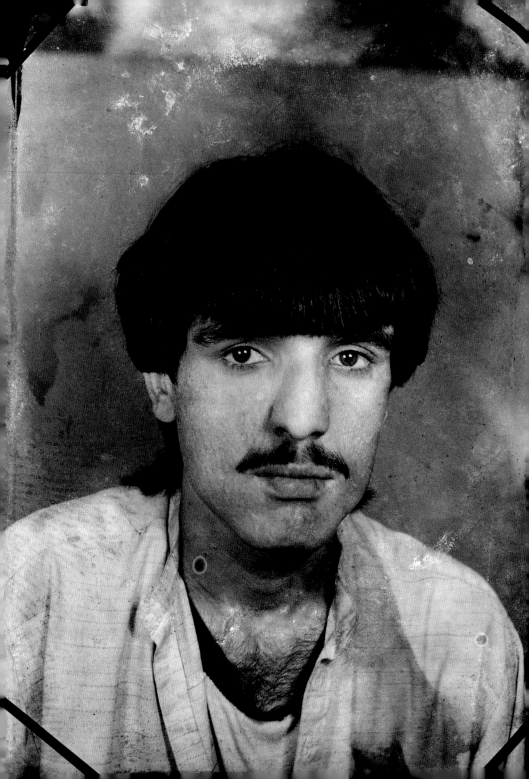

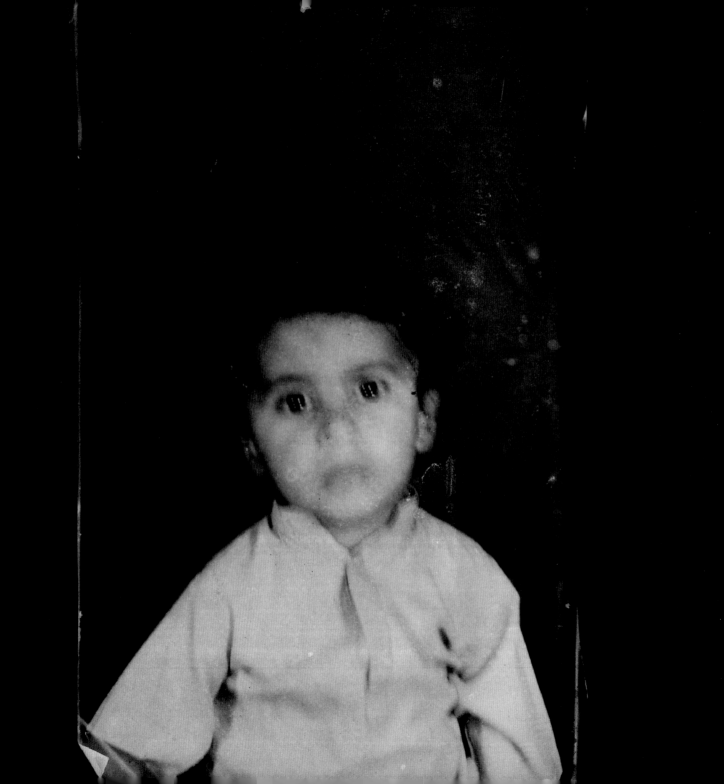

TO KABUL

As the van climbed up through the narrow canyons, rock slides slowed our
progress. In the high mountains, it swerved to avoid ruts and passing vehicles and
we rolled perilously close to the edge, catching a glimpse of the rusting skeletons
of trucks at the foot of the gorge hundreds of meters below. We swept by children
filling holes in the road who called out for donations to their cause — shrill voices
piercing the air as the small figures vanished in clouds of dust. And as we passed
the makeshift battle positions nestling in the hills I thought of the photograph of
the young Mujahed, Abdul Manam, and imagined him staring out over the land.
At twenty-one, in this picture, he sat, rifle in hand, glaring into the camera with
the defiant and self-assured gaze of youth. His eyes spoke of the jihad and a belief
system which allowed no room for doubt. By the time I met him, eighteen years
had passed and his determined gaze was tempered by time and the births of his
seven children who had never seen their land at peace. Abdul Manam had known
Afghanistan before the jihad and had experienced the country as a society intact.
His own peaceful childhood had been followed by interminable war, which was the
legacy left to his children. Looking into the eyes of his infant son, which were so
much like his, I had wondered about the child's future in the cycle of violence.

One night, in the refugee settlement of Bizen Khel, an old man, Sulfir, had
told us about the village in Afghanistan where he was born. In the evenings, after
his work was done, he said, he would climb to the roof of his home and sit on the
warm brick, sipping his tea, looking out across the village and watching the setting
sun as birds darted through the trees. After living in a refugee camp in Pakistan
for more than a decade his memories of those evenings became so strong that
he was driven to leave three generations of his family behind and return to the
remote mountain village to see if his house still existed as it did in his imagination.
When he arrived on the outskirts of the village, he met a man whom he had known
years before. The man told Sulfir that the house he traveled so far to visit had
survived the communist period but was destroyed during the fighting between

Mujahedin factions. Sulfir could not bear to see the house and village in ruins. He had left the man and turned back immediately, retracing his journey to exile.

As we drew nearer to Kabul, we were frequently stopped and searched at Taliban checkpoints. When the Pol-e Charki prison came into view, conversation in the van suddenly died away and travelers of all ages sat motionless, transfixed by the sight of the place. In their closed expressions was the knowledge that thousands of Afghans, many of them innocent, had been killed during the communist era in this jail notorious for civilian torture and murder.

I thought of my last trip to Kabul in 1996 when the Mujahedin government was still in power. There had been heavy fighting along the route from Jalalabad to Kabul and I had flown into the city with the Red Cross. I arrived in the afternoon and went to the UNHCR, where the director's assistant, an Afghan named Manawer, offered to drive me around to get a sense of the city. In a gleaming white Landcruiser he recounted the history of the areas and the buildings we passed. He talked about his own childhood, how he had wandered the streets of the city at night, enraptured by the sight of the grand movie houses and the elegantly dressed couples strolling the lighted boulevards with the shadowy backdrop of the mountains in the distance. He and his family had fled to the north during the Mujahedin civil war and had returned two years later to find Kabul in ruins. As we drove past abandoned villas pockmarked by bullet holes and mortar damage and into the south of the city, we heard rocket fire in the distance. Soon rockets had begun to fall in the area in front of us. The busy street was instantly abandoned. Manawer turned and sped down the avenue away from the blasts. He explained that life in Kabul was lived between rocket attacks.

By this time the van had almost arrived at the center of Kabul and the travelers were preparing for their arrival. We were driving through the Makrorian section, a residential neighborhood which had been the front line during fighting between rival Mujahedin factions. At that time the apartment blocks had served as military bases, but since then their owners had returned and drying laundry covered the rocket craters while children played in the rubble. The van stopped and I clambered out with Abdul Sattar into the streets, reconciling ourselves to the sense of having moved from witness to participant.

Although there had been many checkpoints on the outskirts of the city, most of the Taliban forces were concentrated on the front line defending Kabul against Commander Massoud's Mujahedin forces near Bamiyan. Within the city, the Taliban often traveled without weapons to demonstrate their sense of ease with the citizens and Kabul's acceptance of the Taliban version of Sheria law. Along the Jada Maiwand, Kabul's main artery, an eerie calm prevailed, and a new bazaar was thriving between bombed out buildings.

We had arranged to stay in an Afghan relief organization run by friends of Abdul Sattar, but it had been impossible to send a message from Peshawar to Kabul and we arrived unannounced. We were greeted by the house attendant, a short wiry man with the dignified Mongolian features of the Hazaras who introduced himself as Alhamrat. He left us in one of the rooms while he went to fetch a coal stove before going off to prepare tea. The journey and cold of the high altitude had sapped our energy, and I rested in the warmth while Abdul Sattar began his prayers by my side.

The next day we took a rickshaw to the Demazaing area of Kabul which had been the seat of government during the communist regime. The huge palace on a promontory overlooking the city remains magnificent even in ruins with the ornate oval windows of the upper stories open to the sky. Walking beside the palace we could see inside where the great rooms had been blasted away and red crosses emblazoned across the walls warned passers-by that the ground inside was still mined. From where we stood Abdul Sattar pointed out battle positions on the horizon including the bunker from which the Taliban laid siege to the palace. He spoke of strongholds, front lines, government forces and zones of engagement, how nearly a hundred workers from the Russian center had been massacred in a surprise attack. In this area one of the Mujahedin factions had laid twenty-five thousand mines in one night in an attempt to stop the Taliban from marching into Kabul. The Taliban entered the city by another route, but the mines remained.

As we walked back along the boulevard in the evening chill, we could see that several families had reclaimed their homes. The sound of children playing resounded within the crumbling walls, and a path marked with white splashes of paint indicated the safe route through the minefield. Abdul Sattar had worked with a mine-clearing organization and knew that it took months to remove mines that had been laid in a matter of hours. While he worked, he told me, he often met children searching for wood. The safe areas of Kabul had long since been stripped of trees, and children had begun crossing mined areas to retrieve slivers of kindling. When he warned them about the danger, they said they would rather be blown up than die of cold.

The following morning Abdul Sattar went to visit the family of the woman who would become his third wife. He already supported a household in Peshawar which had thirty-three members. There was his forty-one-year-old first wife, his second wife, who was twenty-one, and a series of children, parents and members of the extended family. Now he would marry a girl of fourteen. She had seen Abdul Sattar when he visited her family and set her heart upon becoming his wife. Her parents understood his reservations regarding their daughter's youth, but told him that the younger generation, from whom this girl might choose her husband, had lost their sense of religion and respect for women. They were born into a warring society and had developed an aggressive response to the world around them. Without the gifts of education and a thoughtful regard for Islam there was little that those men could offer a bride. In such times, she and her family preferred to wed themselves to a respected member of the community from whom they could expect emotional and financial security. The marriage would bind husband to wife and bring two households together. As the families merged, Abdul Sattar would assume responsibility for the care of his bride's parents when they grew old.

While Abdul Sattar was occupied, I walked alone through the streets marking how the Taliban edicts had changed the feel of Kabul. The open squares were no longer filled with children and their kites. The cinemas had been closed and no melodic Dari music drifted through the streets. The Taliban had condemned these idle pleasures, saying they took up time better spent meditating on Islam. The windows of the houses had been bricked up to prevent passers-by from catching a fleeting glimpse of a woman. On the rare occasions when I passed a woman in the streets, she was covered in a *burkha*, a head to toe shroud with lace grille over the eyes, and following several steps behind a male relative. Women had become dark apparitions gliding through the streets without identity.

I thought of the remarkable women I had met in the Afghan refugee villages of Pakistan. Mina Atai, a jovial resident of Akora Khattak, was a teacher and graduate of Kabul University. When the Taliban fired her and turned her daughters away from school, she packed her family's belongings and left for

Fateh Khan

Said Mohammed and his daughter Lima

Ibrahim

Pakistan where the children were enrolled in school and she volunteered as a social worker in the camp. Hundreds of women who were the sole providers for their families had been told to leave their jobs and stay at home. Unable to support their families, they fled to Pakistan. Mina Atai helped those like her make the transition to a new land. She spoke to me proudly about Islam and how she had left because the true religion asks that women be educated and respected. One afternoon she told me about a doctor friend who had continued to make her way to the hospital in Kabul to care for her patients. She was stopped by the Taliban in the street and told to return home. When she pleaded with them that she must care for her patients, they beat her. When she refused to submit, they bayoneted her to death.

Another courageous woman, the author of the statement for this book entitled *Our Plight*, lived with her parents in Kabul until the first weeks of Taliban rule. She watched women and girls thrown out of their offices and schools and told her parents she was leaving the country and traveled alone to the Pakistani border with only a few rupees and no prospect for a job or place to live. Several months later, when we met, she had already learned English and had found a job, and was supporting herself and the brothers and sisters sent to live with her. When she wrote the statement, though she had been threatened by the Taliban for her outspokenness and bravery, she was determined to put her name to it. But she finally accepted that to use her name would put her family in Kabul in danger, and that the strength of the message would, in any case, be carried powerfully without it.

When the Taliban entered Kabul in 1996 they had stormed the UN compound where Najibullah, the last communist President of Afghanistan had been given asylum for four years. The Taliban castrated, then executed Najibullah and his brother before hanging their bodies on public display from the concrete stansion of a police post at a busy crossroads, where they remained for three days. I had been haunted by the photographs of these two dead men, their feet dangling above the ground and their bloodied faces hanging limply to one side, which had been published all over the world. Standing before the site, eighteen months later, I could describe the red and white candy-striped podium perched in the middle of the square, but nothing I could say or write, no photograph I could have taken, could have encompassed the hidden emotional power of the scene. If I thought that coming to this symbolic place would clarify something, I now realized that this journey to the scene of destruction would offer no solutions, only raise more questions. I had begun it with the conviction that from the city I would find out more about the condition of the people. Instead of finding answers at the source, I had stepped into a maze which forced me to wander through the city, the past and the present mingling into one. Everywhere I turned in Kabul, I met contradictions. Just before reaching the police post, I passed a mosque where the Taliban were coming and going from their prayers. How was it that they could go so devoutly to prayer only to come out into the streets and act with such brutality?

That night Abdul Sattar and I were invited to dine at the home of his friend Aziz Kakar. When we stopped at the government offices to pick up an invited minister, the power was out and the building was dark but for an office lit by a candle. As we waited for the minister to emerge a man introduced himself as an assistant minister. When he learned that I had traveled from the United States to Pakistan and that my grandfather was a Muslim, he was pleased to think an American might see his perspective. He was proud of the security the Taliban had brought to Kabul, and bragged about how the Taliban were teaching the Afghans Islam. He said that non-Muslims were not forced to comply with Sheria law, but that since my grandfather was a Muslim, I should learn and embrace Islam. When I came to believe with blind faith, then I would understand that there are some things which lie beyond my comprehension, for they are the will of Allah.

I asked him about Najibullah's death and he told me that Najibullah was responsible for the deaths of thousands of innocent Afghans, that he had ordered people crushed to death by trucks. The hanging and the three-day display of the bodies was intended to admonish the community. During that time, he said, people had come forward to say Najibullah had been responsible for the deaths of their fathers, husbands and friends. Many of them had been so angry that they wanted to beat the dead bodies, but the Taliban had not allowed it. He said Najibullah was a puppet of the communists and not a true Muslim, and that he would not have received an Islamic burial if the people of his village had not come to bring the bodies home for a Muslim ceremony.

This idea of teaching people through exhibitions of violence reminded me of the case of Ghulam Mohammed, a man who murdered a pregnant woman and her three small children in the course of a botched robbery. Eventually, he had been caught and found guilty of the crime. In a field, in public, he had then been placed before Mohammed Alif, the husband of the slain woman. Armed with a Kalashnikov, Mohammed Alif was given the choice of forgiving Ghulam Mohammed or taking his life. He opted for the latter. The photograph of the murderer's bullet ridden body lying in the dirt surrounded by a crowd of Taliban fighters had once again been published in the world press.

I asked the assistant minister about the incident and he said that in an Islamic society those who kill must be put to death because if they were allowed to live, they might kill again. It was the responsibility of a good Muslim to kill a murderer, just as those who speak against Islam should be killed. He said it was the duty of the Taliban to protect and instruct the people against the evils of straying from Islam. I knew from my conversations with Abdul Sattar that forgiveness was one of the highest callings of Islam. But making the husband kill the murderer brought the responsibility for taking a life to rest upon his soul.

The assistant minister said he knew what the West thought of the Taliban but how could they criticize Afghanistan when Western atrocities had been visited on so many so far afield. He remembered the days of the jihad against the Soviets when Afghans thought Americans felt a genuine empathy for their position, but when Afghanistan was no longer of strategic interest, they were abandoned to their fate. He told me people in the West had been seduced by materialism and their life obstructed the path of the pious. Turning to leave with a condescending smile, he said that if the Americans were not doing well enough to help his people now perhaps the Afghans could take up a collection to send them some assistance.

That night at Aziz Kakar's house, I sat drinking my tea quietly watching as the Taliban minister's acolytes jockeyed for position, ingratiating themselves in a bid to win favor with the powerful man. Aziz Kakar's young son crouched in the corner of the room, refilling the minister's cup until he covered it with his hand to indicate that he had drunk enough. Then the son circled the group collecting cups, carefully observing protocol and honoring the hierarchies within the group.

A few minutes later, Aziz Kakar's father entered the room, impressive in his swaying *silvar* and turban, and we rose to greet the old man. He sat in one corner opposite the minister where he could survey the room, subtly motioning to the young men of the household as they attended to the guests throughout the evening. After a lavish banquet, the father addressed us. With great poise and authority he related his experiences under the communists and then during the Mujahedin era. He had been a successful businessman before joining the Mujahedin government where he had become a respected minister. He spoke of mistakes the Mujahedin had made, and of the people's sorrow when the movement had failed. He said that one of their greatest errors had been to reject the intellectuals and those capable of stabilizing of the government. If the Taliban engaged with wise men to stabilize the government, then they would be able to sustain themselves. In a concerned but respectful voice he concluded with a plea for the Taliban to honor the residents of Kabul.

With his emotional speech at an end, all eyes turned back to the Taliban minister who accepted the statement with the correct degree of gracious appreciation. And yet, watching his expression, it seemed he was going through the formalities of office without having heard a word. As the curfew drew closer, the minister rose, gathering his flowing garments together, and bade his farewell. He embraced the old man before leading us out of the room into the bitter night. We climbed into the jeep and braced ourselves as the driver made a hurried return to the city center.

At the outer gate of the mission where we were staying we knocked on the sheet metal and Alhamrat unbolted the entrance. Not wanting to waste fuel in the lantern by his side, he had stood waiting for us in the dark. He lit the lantern and wished us a safe trip for the following day before handing the glow to Abdul Sattar and stepping away into the darkness. At home, he would be greeted by children who would hurry him to the warmth of the family room. In winter, the families of Kabul gather in one room where a coal stove is placed beneath a table in the center. A broad blanket is then spread on the table top, its fringes ranging to the corners of the room. As the streets darken and the chill of night takes hold, several generations of a family come to the communal room to slip beneath the coal-warmed blanket for the night. In the morning they leave its sanctuary and return to the city, carrying with them those hours of reprieve.

Malang Jan

A rose can come from a thorn, a thorn can come from a rose.

Shahria

Baharam and his son Muradi

Sisters, Sima and Shahima

Salim, Padan Khan and Sayejan

Abdul Ghafur's daughter Hadija

Sharif Khan

Sharif Khan

Shafiqa

Nour Ahmed and his sleeping great-grandson

FAREWELL

I spent my last afternoon in Peshawar with Abdul Sattar and his family. We sat in their garden sipping sweet and milky Pakistani tea while his children played a boisterous game of cricket. A visiting uncle sat smiling broadly by my side. We talked of the coming marriage and laughed about our return trip from Afghanistan when, because our van broke down, we were forced to spend the night in a *chaikhane* at the border post with hundreds of stranded travelers who huddled grumpily together through the night.

As the day shortened, the children surrendered their game and returned to the house while the uncle limped across the lawn to his bed. It was late when I finally took my bicycle and prepared to go back to where I was staying, but Abdul Sattar insisted on keeping me company. As we rode side by side, I focused on the cool breeze and the chatter of villagers' voices fading in and out of the dark. From time to time a cigarette was lit and the face of a villager was etched out of the night.

Saying goodbye to Abdul Sattar in front of my door I realized how much we had come to mean to one another and how much I had learned from this man. He had opened a window to his country and the faith which he embraced. He told me that he had never worked with someone from the West in whom he had witnessed such a duality. He said that he saw that I was born, raised, and educated in the West but that my feeling for others and my spirit remained in the East.

As I lay down for the last time in the Peshawar night, I thought back to a trip I had made with Abdul Sattar to Chitral. It was during the frigid onset of winter and we had traveled over the mountains on our way to the northern refugee village at Khairabad. Soon the mountain pass would be blocked by snow and passage in and out of the area would be impossible until the spring thaw. I had been sitting in my bed, swathed in blankets, writing about the day's events, with a kerosene heater clicking away by my side sending volumes of smoke into the room, when from the courtyard outside came the words: "Allah akbar," Allah is great.

At first the voice, resonant and deep, seemed foreign. I peered into the near-darkness where a group of men were huddled together, facing away from me towards the northwest and Mecca. The voice was that of Abdul Sattar but it was so transformed that I hardly recognized it. He stood before the group leading them in prayer. Following his supplication, the men bent forward in unison and, with a further intonation, crouched to their knees and, finally, forward to rest their foreheads upon the ground. The social divisions between the men, so conspicuous during the course of the day, had vanished: the owner of the hotel stood beside the cook and the boy who cleaned the toilets; the other residents of the guest-house were gathered by them, and I witnessed the beauty of the religion. At that moment it became clear that in Afghanistan I was not confronting injustices within the core message of Islam but, rather, within a society fractured by war and power which could no longer see its way clear to a charitable posture in the world.

Abdul Sattar once told me that there were some things more important than a person's self interest. For him, as for many Afghans, those elements were Islam, family, and the bones buried in a village many hundreds of miles away from these homes in exile. As the world spins impossibly out of control around them, Afghans look further inward, narrowing their scope of vision to their own friends and families to find the spirit that will sustain them.

When two bulls fight, the leg of the calf is broken.

Abdul Kalan's *madrasa*

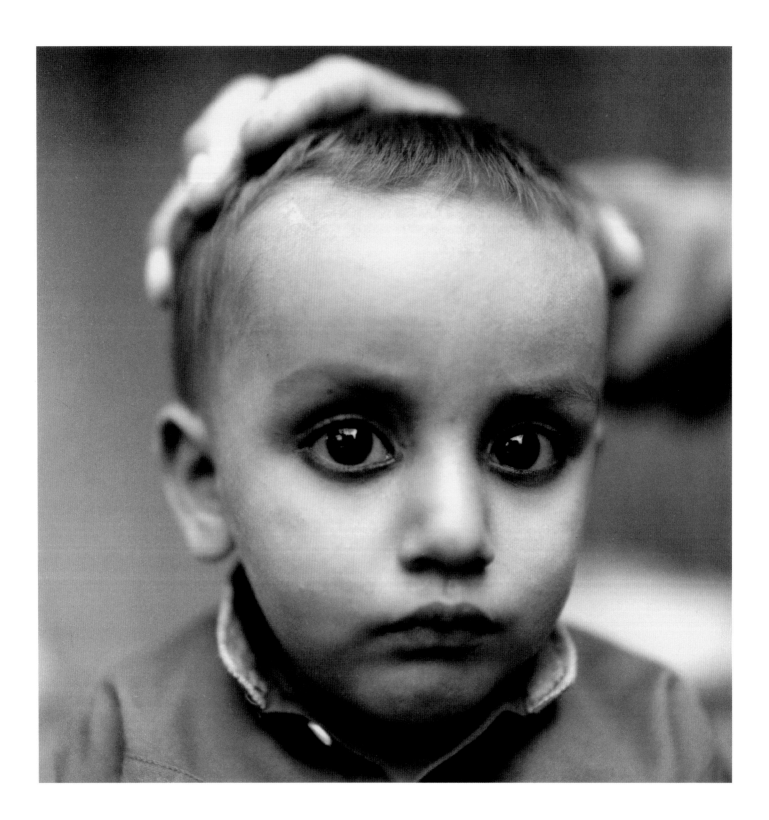

Afghan children born in exile (pages 222–243)

Koran in girl's hands, Abdul Kalan's *madrasa*

ACKNOWLEDGMENTS

I am enormously grateful to the Afghan villagers of Akhora Khattak, Badabare, Ghazi, Ghandi Khan Khail, Khairabad, Miram Shah, Nasir Bagh, Timergara, and Urghuch who invited me into their homes, their hearts and their country. They taught me that there is more than sadness and destruction in Afghanistan.

Abdul Sattar—who allowed me to see my grandfather's living faith, offering me his friendship and caring without which there would be no book. It was an honor to travel with you.

Walter Keller—I will never be able to express the deep sense of gratitude I feel towards you for having the courage to stand beside me, to collaborate with me and to engage the material. You give your artists unprecedented license to follow their vision. For your extraordinary generosity, encouragement and hope, I thank you.

Hans Werner Holzwarth—I never cease to marvel at your insight. In you I have found the wonderful melding of brilliant designer and dear friend. Thank you for your grace, your counsel and your contemplation; and for the warmth that you, Angelika Stricker and Fritz have lavished upon me.

Liz Jobey—You sat by my side and invested yourself fully in the text. I feel privileged to have worked with you. Thank you for sharing your vast knowledge of the medium and for the gift of your humor and energy which led me through the most difficult period.

Angelika Stricker—Your considered compilation of the historical text, coupled with your understanding of the region proved invaluable. Thank you for exploring the issues with me and for caring so deeply for the project.

Jodi Hauptman, Sunny Lenz and Laura McPhee—At various stages you each lent me your years of understanding and insight with sensitive readings of the text. When I had lost perspective, you gave me a center. During two weeks in Virginia, I drew from the spirits of Robert and Sunny Lenz. As their life's work has formed my priorities, I can think of no place more fitting to finish the book. I hope to give back a fraction of what you two have given your community.

Gerd Steidl—Your remarkable dedication to printing and your sympathy for the artists with whom you work is reflected in the power of your creations. I am grateful to have the chance to build upon the connection forged during our last work and to have found someone who can bring the message home with resounding clarity.

Gert Schwab—Your dexterous and precise handling of the separations gave the images luminosity. Thank you for the extraordinary patience and expertise that you have lent, to this book and to *A Sense of Common Ground*.

Peter MacGill—Over the years you have taught me a great deal. Thank you for believing in the work, and for standing by me with your warm enthusiasm and gentle diplomacy. My thanks to dear Kim Jones and the entire staff at PaceWildensteinMacGill.

Martha Schneider—Your joy of life carries into photography enriching the medium. Your efforts and those of Valerie Bruss at the Schneider Gallery are greatly appreciated.

I would like to acknowledge the following people and institutions for their support and encouragement: ACBAR, Afghan Mine Clearance Planning Association for their work in Afghanistan and for providing the children's drawings, Afghan National Coordinating Bureau, Belquis Ahmedy for her strength and foresight, Vince Aletti, Phil Block, Peter Bunnell, Peter Eisenberger, Hamayun Ferhut, Kathy Grove, Maria Morris Hambourg, Buz Hartshorn, Barbara Hitchcock, Human Rights Watch, Toby Jurovics, Koh-I-Noor Foundation, Laboratorium, Leica, The Mother Jones Documentary Program, Northampton Photographic, Jerry and Alicia Ostriker, Sandra Phillips, Polaroid Corporation and the Artist's Support Program, The Princeton Materials Institute, George Reinhart, Jorge Schneider, Steven Shore, Urs Stahel, UNHCR and its staff members, Code Cisse—who welcomed me to his home and family, Hugh Hudson, Ann Carlin, Rupert Coleville—for his tireless work in bringing the Afghan situation to the world, Marie Okabe—for helping to pave the way, Terry Pitzner, Ghaseem Ferdanesh, Anjum Shah, Mustaq and the UNHCR drivers, Tomas Weski, Colin Westerbeck, John and Ruth Wilson.

My gratitude to the SCALO family—Therese Abbt, Marianne Müller, Petra Müller, Pia Rohr, Eveline Sievi, Martin Jäggi, Matthias Läuchli, Oliver Schmidt and Alexis Schwarzenbach who welcomed me in Zurich and New York. What a pleasure it was to be in your company.

At the Steidl, Schwab printing house I would like to thank Bernard Fischer—for moving the project along in all phases, Katja Töpfer—for her collaboration in adjusting the images, Günther Lerbs—for his exacting pre-press work, Ursula Stricker, and the wonderful team of printers who handled these pages with such care: Karl-Heinz Gotthard, Axel Legantke, Andreas Nickel, Günther Rohde, Bernd Schäfer and Christof Staeck.

I have drawn heavily from my family and friends during this period and I hope they know that this work only exists because of their love. You have profoundly affected my life. I am only able to go away because I know that I always have a home with each and every one of you.

My father Abdul Majied Sheikh who is always in my thoughts when we are apart and his wife Seemin Mauladad Sheikh for introducing me to the melody of my culture, Fahd and Farrah Mauladad, Bill and Lisa Koutsoukos, Katie and Emily Lenz for their humor and company during my time at home. Libby Lenz and Marshal Gorham, Gaby and Ali Sheikh, Shela Sheikh, Zaidi and Zeba Sheikh, and to my dear Kiki Post whose love, shared understanding and sanctuary during this year have been a source of joy.

My beloved friends who are an extension of my family: Charlie and Cathy Ashmun, Mike and Virginia Beahan, Leslie Bienen and Tom Brayton, Henry and Leigh Bienen, William and Natalie Bland, John Borsch and Dorothea Dietrich, Greg Clarick and Jodi Hauptman, Marciann Fallon, Ellen Fitzpatrick, Emmet and Edith Gowin, Dr Martin and Ellen Hauptman, Jeff Hoone and Carrie Mae Weems, Mohammed Kalim Husain, Mark Lapore and Laura McPhee, Gina Martinuzzi, Accra Shepp and Alva Rogers, John and Shari Silverstein, David Shrayer and Carol Tate, Carla Williams, and Johanna Wilson.

And finally, to the memory of my mother Nini Sheikh, Lila Southard Lenz, Winthrop C. Lenz and Sheikh Fazal Ilahi who are gone but who I carry with me.

Sheikh Fazal Ilahi's legacy and priorities during his lifetime were clearly delineated in his acts of compassion. In that spirit, the royalties from this publication will be donated to the communities that so generously collaborated with the work.

Fazal Sheikh — The Victor Weeps

Editors: Walter Keller, Liz Jobey
Design: Hans Werner Holzwarth, Berlin
Separations: Gert Schwab/Steidl, Schwab Scantechnik, Göttingen
Production: Steidl, Göttingen

© 1998 for texts and photographs: Fazal Sheikh
© 1998 for the map (p. 14): Hans Werner Holzwarth, Berlin
© 1998 for this edition: Scalo Zurich – Berlin – New York
Head office: Weinbergstrasse 22a, CH-8001 Zurich/Switzerland,
phone 41 1 261 0910, fax 41 1 261 9262, e-mail publishers@scalo.com
Distributed in North America by D.A.P., New York City;
in Europe, Africa and Asia by Thames and Hudson, London;
in Germany, Austria and Switzerland by Scalo.

First Scalo edition 1998
ISBN 3-931141-95-0
Printed in Germany

Sources of the historical overview (p. 15): *Encyclopædia Britannica*, London 1994–1998, *The Encyclopædia of Islam*, Leiden 1960–1989 (new edition), and *Encyclopædia Iranica*, London 1982 ff.
Sources of the quotes (pp. 19, 65): Barnett R. Rubin, *The Search for Peace in Afghanistan*, New Haven and London 1995, and *Report of the U.S. Helsinki Watch Committee*, 1984.

29 1999